LIVING IN
THE THIRD MILLENNIUM

Forecasts to Master your Future

by

Konrad M. Kressley, Ph.D.

Factor Press
PO Box 8888
Mobile, Alabama 36689

ISBN 1-887650-12-1

Publishers Cataloging-in-Publication
Konrad, Kressley.
    Living in the third millennium/Kressley, Konrad
    p. cm.
    ISBN 1-887650-12-1
    1. Social prediction. 2. Economic forecasting. 3. Employment forecasting. I. Title. H61.4.K7488 1998

Typeset by Ronald E. Feuerlein

Table of Contents

Globalization
The Political Agenda of the Next Century
Likely Solutions

YOUR WORK AND CAREER: A Tale of Hazards and
Opportunities

Automation: The Revolution in the Workplace
Human Consequences of the Information Revolution
Yuppies? Fire When Ready
A Visit to the 21st Century Workplace
Can We Learn From Corporate Reorganization?
The End of Work
Learning to Learn: Flexible Education in the 21st
      Century
Lifetime Learning: What You Must Do
Job and Career Choices in the Next Century

WHERE'S MY CHECK? Forecasting Social Security and
Pension Benefits

False Sense of Security?
Pension Plans in Transition
"Do it Yourself" Pensions Arrive
The Uncertain Future of Pensions
Social Security: Rock or Quicksand?
Why Social Security?
Demographics, Automation and the Crisis of the 1980s
Some Myths and Realities
How Come my Check is so Small?
Is Privatization the Answer?
Coming Full Circle in the Next Century

Family Inheritance: A Dubious Nest Egg
Learning to invest
Setting Goals and Making Choices
Hobby Investing for Fun and Profit
Follow the Boomers!
Picking Technology Winners
A Daewoo in your Future? Think Global

Medicine, Science and Technology
Doctor's Orders: The Strange World of Medical
 Economics
From Black Bag Medicine to High Tech Industry
How Much Health Care is Enough?
The Battle of Cost Control
Understanding Managed Care
Medical Occupations in Transition
Clinics of the Future
Baby Boomers, Medicare and the Long Term Care
 Dilemma
So How Do We Pay For It?
Look for National Health Care to Return

You, the Health Care consumer
Lifestyle Choices
Wellness: It Pays to be Healthy

Shape Up or Else?
Aging and Health
Be Your Own Doctor: Investing in Lifetime Health
Fountains of Youth at the Mall?
Is the Doctor Always Right?
The Dawn of Alternative Medicine
Have a Nice Death—The Final Choice

YOUR HOME OR YOUR PIGGY BANK? Housing in the
21st Century

The Baby Boom as Building Boom
Yesterday's Real Estate Fortunes
Demographic Trends and Future Housing Values
21st Century Homes: Factory Direct?
Population Migrations: America on the Move
Housing Options in Later Life
Real Estate Investing in the Third Millennium

NOW THAT YOU KNOW: Facing the Future With Courage
and Confidence

Forecasting the 21st Century Life Cycle
Good Old Days?
Values and Attitudes for the Next Century
Surviving Information Age Overload and Uncluttering
    Life
Your Legacy: The ultimate Future Investment

Preface

"Only the Lead Dog Sees the Landscape."
—Old Eskimo Proverb

Writing this book about the future has been both an adventure and an experience in personal growth. I was forced to confront a changing world and changes that are happening to me. You see, some aspects of the future are truly elating; others, frankly, are depressing. Nevertheless, I prefer to face the future with open eyes and hope that you will share this view as you read on.

Much of the material for *Living in the Third Millennium* originated in my academic research publications and classroom lectures over the past two decades. By working with students, I came to realize that, while corporations, governments and other institutions make extensive use of forecasting, most individuals, like you and I, are unaware of what lies ahead. I then decided to take the mainstream forecasts to answer the cares and concerns of middle Americans at the turn of the new century. This book is the result. Forecasting, by the way, is steadily gaining in accuracy as systematic research in the field of Future Studies matures. As you can imagine, all such literature involves some speculation and educated guesses by the author. I have tried to support all forecasts with a solid empirical basis.

Along the way, I have received generous advice and support. My association with the World Future Society provided me with a wealth of imaginative and balanced sources of information. Some individuals also stand out. One of them is Jean Barilla, whose own efforts inspired me to write. My daughter Regina Kressley gently stoked my motivation over several years. Among my colleagues, there is Dr. Sam Fisher, who helped with word processing technology, Dr. Ed Bunnell, who furthered my interest in Future Studies, and Dr. Roma Hanks, who has been a mentor for aging issues. I am also indebted to my chairman, Dr. Robert Barrow, for support of the research which went into the text. Robert Bahr of Factor Press gave me invaluable advice on how to structure the manuscript. Finally, I am most grateful to Patricia Janssen of Tulane University, who patiently edited several drafts of this book.

—Konrad M. Kressley
Mobile, Alabama
1998

Introduction: Why Be Concerned About The Future?

The doctor has great news: Thanks to tofu, oat bran and daily YMCA workouts, you can expect to live long beyond the age of your parents! Meanwhile, back at the office, the boss has hired a management wizard to help him downsize the staff. There are whispers that the next generation of computers could make your job obsolete, putting you on the street long before retirement age. Later, at home, you turn on the TV to hear a pompous commentator proclaim that Social Security and Medicare will soon go broke, and that the politicians are calling on us to take responsibility for our own retirement. So, what do you do?

Tomorrow's News Today

Well, you're not alone. Future trends dictate to all of us, but most harshly to those who are unprepared. Living in the

Third Millennium is a road map to the future, revealing what lies ahead and suggesting strategies for mastering life's problems in the next century. Unknown to many of us, there is a large and well developed Forecasting Industry which caters to the world of business and government. Do forecasts work? You'd better believe it! Corporations and public officials spend fortunes to study the future. Significant forecasts over the past 20 and 30 years have proven to be remarkably correct in terms of what is happening today. It's a wonder that individuals have failed to exploit this valuable guide to chart their personal future. Who knows, the higher ups may well want to keep this information to themselves.

This book summarizes the consensus forecasts for the next decades, pointing out perils and opportunities for people like you and me. The experts agree that certain developments are inevitable and will impact all of us. These are demographics, economic trends and continued technology advances. In a nutshell, lower birth rates and longer life spans, coupled with the Baby Boom phenomenon, will produce a much larger elderly population in the next century. At the same time, years of accumulated debt and rising age-based entitlements will slow down the economy. Continued globalization of economic life will create both benefits and hardships. What's good for Wall Street is not always good for Main Street. Finally, the computer-based technology revolution, referred to as the information age by futurists, has not yet run its course; it will change our lives significantly and make many occupations obsolete. Some futurists, like Jeremy Rifkin, even talk about "the end of work!"

Are You Ready?

Knowing about the future is not enough. Successive chapters reveal how various aspects of life will be changed and how you can anticipate and cope with what lies ahead. Chapter 2, Your Work and Career, is chilling, but it also offers hope. Those stylish Yuppies, now in middle management, are vulnerable targets for corporate downsizing. As the "information revolution" sweeps away traditional occupations, those "in the know" can jump on the band wagon in terms of retraining and career changes. Previous generations worked their way through college; you'll need to "college your way through work." You'll also be surprised to learn that some of the most promising occupations of the future, like mortuary management, have little to do with high tech. The ability to communicate, good people skills and a willingness to change are among the most important lessons to be learned.

If you're worried about the security of your retirement, you have good reason to be. The growing elderly population and pressure to balance the budget will trim future Social Security and Medicare benefits. Chapter 3, Where's My Check? describes how this once generous system will be gradually reduced to a bare bones safety net. Meanwhile, pensions face an austere future, as business seeks a way to preserve profits by reducing its future retirement obligations. If the future of entitlements is dismal, the answer can be found in Chapter 4, Investment. All of us need to learn how to invest, using the future as a guide. Here's your chance to cash in on the trends described in other chapters. To begin with, follow the Boomers when it comes to picking growth opportunities. But you don't have to be a financial wizard to meet your goals. There are more than enough stable, secure investment vehicles. Are you adventurous? Then, try picking future technology winners or cruise the international market place. There's a Daewoo in your future!

Taking Care of Yourself

Chapter 5, To Your Health, describes the rise of the corporate medical industry and how technology will transform medical practice in the next century. There's both good news and bad news. On the one hand, we will witness gene therapy, artificial organs and many other medical advances. On the other hand, increased costs will be managed only by rationing drugs, hospital stays and surgical procedures. Our most serious future problem, perhaps, will come in meeting the health care needs of retired baby boomers which will start around 2020. You can expect to bear a much larger share of your health care costs in the future; terminal health care bills could gobble up your retirement nest eggs and inheritance.

Fortunately, there's help if you become an informed and active medical consumer. Chapter 6, Be Your Own Doctor, points out that most folks think of their body like a car or a machine which breaks down from time to time. The doctor then cuts it open and fixes the parts. Curiously, we perform meticulous preventive maintenance on our cars, but neglect our bodies until a crisis arrives. This chapter offers tips for maintaining lifetime health. Individual responsibility is the bottom line. Along the way, we need to become more skeptical of the medical establishment, with its newly discovered corporate profit mentality. Some of the most dramatic developments will take place outside the traditional medical establishment. Look for "fountains of youth" at the mall, featuring nutriceuticals and a host of devices to make us slim, sleep better, regrow hair and improve our sex lives. Meanwhile, acupuncture, meditation therapy and other techniques of alternative medicine from the Asian tradition will enter the mainstream. Finally, death, itself, will be redefined so that individuals will gain some control over the time and circumstances of their demise.

Coming Home

The next century's demographic transition will have a dramatic effect on America's housing. Chapter 7, Your Home or Your Piggy Bank, predicts that real estate markets will be turned on their heads as growing numbers of senior citizens abandon suburban single family homes and flock to easily accessible apartments and condominiums. You may want to reconsider your real estate investments after reading this chapter.

Meanwhile, we will feel the influence of technology as factories start to churn out custom designed modular homes. Population migrations from the Northeast and North Central regions to the Sunbelt will accelerate as affluent Baby Boomers reach retirement age. If you live in one of the "losing" states, like Pennsylvania, brace yourself for an economic downturn. But Floridians, Texans and other Sunbelt residents, who now gloat about the influx, should realize that they will face crushing social support and health care cost burdens for these aging migrants in the not-too-distant future! Under these circumstances, real estate investing promises to be a real adventure in the next century.

The concluding chapter, Now that You Know, is a challenge to rethink your life in terms of the 21st century world. Our basic premise is that many values and attitudes, which made good sense in earlier times, won't serve us well in the post-industrial information age. Consider the forecasts of a longer life span coupled with uncertain employment and retirement income. Chilling, isn't it? Unless, of course, society and individuals rethink such issues of work, leisure, and the distribution of economic rewards. In that case, gains in longevity and robust life-long health create exciting prospects for creative and bountiful personal lives. The choice is up to you, and there's no better way to get ready for the future than by reading this book!

Chapter 1
THE ART OF FORECASTING:
What Lies Ahead?

When considering the future, most folks immediately think about palm readers, Jean Dixon, or the Psychic Hot Line. Others engage in furtive encounters with the occult, calling on astrology for romantic and financial insights. Then there's the genre of science fiction, which depicts a future of leotard-clad astronauts crossing the universe to meet furry ape-like creatures in other galaxies. While these have enormous entertainment value, they should not be confused with serious efforts to study the future.

Rise of the Forecasting Industry

Since forecasting enterprises don't overtly advertise, much of the public is unaware that this significant industry has evolved over the past several decades. It began in obscure government agencies, universities, and arcane "think tanks." The invention of the computer played an enormous role in creating the art of forecasting; it allowed researchers to assemble and analyze unprecedented amounts of information which, up to then, had boggled the human mind. Today, futurists are both respected and influential, particularly among the high level-insiders who rely upon their work.

Where do you find a futurist? Experts of forecasting and future studies organized to form the World Future Society in 1966. The society conducts annual conventions and publishes a widely-circulated magazine, *The Futurist.* There is also a rich literature of other future-oriented books, journals, and internet offerings. Some prestigious educational institutions, like the University of Houston, now offer graduate degree programs in this emerging field. Some futurists, whose work we'll look at later, have achieved public recognition. Chief among them are the late Herman Kahn of the Hudson Institute, Alvin and Heidi Toffler, who wrote the best sellers *Future Shock and The Third Wave,* and John Naisbitt, author of *Megatrends.* Meanwhile, countless other forecasters contribute through their work at more pedestrian tasks. For example, city planners, corporate strategists, and forecasters in the federal government's advisory councils are largely invisible; yet they contribute to the rich and growing storehouse of impending developments and consequences. We may take their work for granted, but they nevertheless shape our future.

Care to visit with some futurists? There are now several hundred individual consultants and firms which offer forecasting services. The *Institute for the Future*, based in Menlo Park, California, is typical. The Institute's staff consists of about 20 affiliates, most of whom hold doctoral degrees in a wide range of fields including engineering, business management, and anthropology. Like other forecasting firms, they originally employed only experts from science and engineering but, as time went on, they realized the need for social and behavioral researchers as well. Staffers share two important characteristics: First, they have open minds, which gives them the capacity to see beyond their own disciplines; second, the ability to communicate and synthesize ideas with their colleagues. The atmosphere ranges between a research university and a consulting firm. Unfortunately, you won't find many of them at company headquarters. Most staffers operate in the emerging "virtual environment," which means that their offices are at home, on the road, or wherever they choose to switch on their lap-top computers. While a certain amount of face-to-face contact is still necessary, this type of organization depends more on electronic communication than weekly staff meetings. We'll take a closer look at this phenomenon in Chapter 2, which describes work and careers in the next century.

Most such institutes publish newsletters, or bulletins that provide corporate and institutional subscribers with 5- or 10-year general forecasts. They also provide customized forecasts for their clients. Typically, corporate and institutional executives want to know about threats and opportunities posed by emerging technologies. You don't want to get blindsided by unforesen events, so a counter-intuitive, outside opinion may be worth its weight in gold. For instance, one corporation wants to know how interactive radio, due in 2005, will affect its business. Another firm, which had long manufactured steel file cabinets, asked for ideas on how to adapt its product line to the "paperless office" of the future. By the way, issues of marketing, consumer taste, and customer service receive as much consideration as technologies of the future.

How do they forecast the future?

As you are now aware, these expert forecasters do not rely on a crystal ball. They use sophisticated techniques, combining the latest scientific know-how with human insight and experience. Let's review some of their most widely used approaches to forecast the future.

Trend Extrapolation goes on the assumption that the future is essentially a continuation of the past. The Census Bureau plots population growth projections on existing growth rates, while businessmen determine the future demand for products on the record of past sales figures. Trend extrapolation is the simplest and most logical forecasting technique and relies heavily on computer analysis of statistical information. While it is extremely accurate in the short run, unexpected development in the more distant future can flaw the projections. In the early 1950s, for instance, doctors could predict the number of polio cases with remarkable accuracy from year to year. As you can imagine, the subsequent discovery of the Salk and Sabin polio vaccines made those long-range forecasts meaningless.

Expert Forecasting relies heavily on the insights and intuitions of the most knowledgeable people in a given field. Leonardo DaVinci was celebrated for his scientific and technological vision many centuries ago. More recently, the late oceanographer Jacques Cousteau was frequently asked to make predictions about the world's marine life, while Lee Iacocca is consulted about the automotive future. Despite their impeccable credentials, all experts have personal limitations, vested interests, and biases which tend to distort their analyses. To overcome this problem and to pool the collective wisdom of experts, the **Delphi** technique was developed. Here, a " think tank," like the Rand Corporation in California, assembles a panel of experts and requires them to write answers to specific questions about the future. Once this is done, their forecasts are made available to all other panelists, who then embark on a revised forecast based on what they learned from their colleagues. A critical feature of the Delphi technique is that all forecasts are anonymous, so that the experts' judgement will not be clouded by professional rivalries, cliques, and interpersonal relationships found in any such group. After a number of these cycles, the collective wisdom of the group usually produces some meaningful consensus.

Leading Indicators are another common forecasting tool. Popularized in John Naisbitt's book *Megatrends*, this approach assumes that a small number of innovators start trends which eventually "snowball," as they catch on with more and more people. For example, Paris fashion shows greatly determine the fashions that will be found in boutiques from Dusseldorf to Dubuque; California conceives youth fads; and Silicon Valley initiates computer innovations. The trick, of course, is to identify leading indicators early on so that forecasts for a larger society are possible. This principle applies not only to fads and fashions but to social, economic, and political innovations as well. Just as people choose their outfits based on what those around them are wearing, business and government institutions carefully check out their counterparts before making major decisions. You might say it's a "herd instinct."

Finally, the concept of leading indicators plays a major role in economic forecasting, where monthly statistics on housing starts, for instance, would also generate forecasts of employment, durable goods sales, and related economic trends.

As you can imagine, the most effective forecasting is done by combining various techniques to create synergy. We know intuitively that a variety of trends are interacting simultaneously. Forecasters try to determine these interrelationships by using the technique of **Cross-Impact Analysis**, which utilizes highly sophisticated, statistical methods. One can observe the "ripple effects" when a jump in Middle East petroleum prices affects our gasoline consumption, car sales, and airline ticket prices. On a larger scale, scientists use computer models to plot global climate change by calculating the interaction of factors such as population growth, economic activity, and emission of pollutants. Now you know where the theory of global warming came from.

While statistics and computers have their place, there is still no substitute for the intuition and imagination of the human mind. If anything, forecasts based on hard, statistical facts give creative futurists something to work with and relate to a larger context. This is the essence of **Scenarios**, where futurists combine a number of forecasts into a hypothetical course of events. Scenario, a theatrical term, can also be described as a "story line" or plot of future events. Defense planners have a similar technique, called **Contingency Planning**, where all possible outcomes of a military action are calculated. During the Cold War, Pentagon planners once actually concocted a scenario of nuclear defeat and prepared contingency plans for a surrender to the Russians! While this example may seem absurd, other scenarios have indeed become reality.

Believe it or not, the literature of **Science Fiction** is also gaining acceptance as a forecasting tool. It appears that some of the best writers, like the late astronomer Carl Sagan, are able to combine solid scientific knowledge with fertile imaginations. The Frenchman Jules Verne thrilled his readers with prophetic tales of space travel and submarine adventures well before the turn of the century. And consider the work of Aldous Huxley, the British novelist who published *Brave New World* in 1932. Looking several hundred years into the future, Huxley envisioned a world where science reigns: Human reproduction, divorced from sexuality, is handled in laboratory test tubes; meanwhile, mood-altering drugs keep everyone in a constant state of happiness. In fact, many of these technologies are already available, and Huxley erred only in underestimating the pace of change. Currently, innovations in the field of **Virtual Reality** are particularly close to recent science fiction literature. More about this later.

Skeptics sometimes ask about the accuracy of forecasts and whether they are really worth the high fees charged by professional futurists. The success of the industry should be evidence enough. In fact, a number of studies show the growing success rate of forecasting over the last several decades. Edward Cornish, President of the World Future Society, recently evaluated a set of forecasts made in the inaugural issue of *The Futurist* in 1967. Out of 34 forecasts, there were 23 hits and 11 misses in 1997, just 30 years later. The futurists were right about such things as use of artificial organ parts, growth in agricultural production, and the common use of drugs to treat psychiatric disorders. They erred in predicting widespread availability of desalinated sea water, three-dimensional TV, and that most urban people would live in high-rise buildings. What is the future of future studies? While earlier forecasting focused mainly on science, technology, and economics, the current crop of futurists also takes great interest in issues of culture, society, human development, and spirituality.

What Lies Ahead?

We can now draw on these forecasting techniques to create some scenarios of what life will be like for Americans in the first half of the 21st century. Three interrelated factors are the driving force: population or demographic trends, advances in technology, and future economic developments. There is a broad consensus among futurists of what will inevitably happen. Government policies, unfortunately, are wild cards since they reflect shifting public opinion in response to other developments. Now, let's take a closer look.

I. Population Trends: A Grayer and More Diverse America

According to the Census Bureau, America's population growth is slowing down from year to year. At the end of the 20th century, we are hovering at roughly 265 million, with a one percent growth rate each year. Immigration from abroad currently is the single largest source of additional people. This is in sharp contrast to earlier periods of our history, such as the colonial and frontier period, when population growth skyrocketed due to high birth rates and successive waves of immigrants. Actually, modest growth or stagnation is common to most industrialized countries, while population continues to rise in the Third World. The populations of some countries in Northern Europe are actually declining at this time!

While the total U.S. population is stabilizing, dramatic changes are evolving in the age composition. Most notably, we are currently experiencing a "graying" of the population. Figure 1 shows what's happening in terms of the nation's median age. Historians tell us that America was once a country of young people. The average life span in colonial times scarcely exceeded the mid-thirties. Only the lucky few could expect to reach today's average life expectancy of mid- to-late 70's. The immigrants were also overwhelmingly young people, which further enhanced the nation's youthful image in the past.

A number of factors contributed to these changes in the national age equation. Medical science made enormous strides in protecting us from the fatal diseases which regularly claimed large numbers of children and young adults in previous centuries (check older tombstones in your local cemetery for the heartbreaking evidence). Improved sanitation, nutrition, and more wholesome lifestyles have also added years to our lives. Environmental pollution was often much worse during early phases of industrial development in our country.

Once children had a better chance of surviving infancy, parents were more likely to limit their number. Economic and technological changes also affected the population. Early agricultural and industrial societies prized children as obedient and reliable field hands and factory workers. But the advent of agricultural mechanization and industrial mass production demanded a smaller, more highly skilled population; today's child requires extensive training and education prior to entering the work force. No wonder today's parents consider youngsters a burden, rather than an asset, to the family's livelihood. Finally, parents no longer look to their children as sources of support in

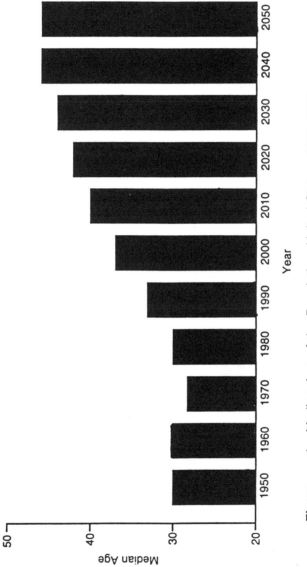

Figure 1 Median Age of the Population: United States, 1950–2050 (*Source:* U.S. Bureau of the Census, *Current Population Reports*, Series P-25, No. 1018. Washington, DC: U.S. Government Printing Office, 1989.)

later life. Pension plans and government entitlement programs have largely replaced filial responsibility in modern society. Having kids is still a wonderful idea, but hardly a profitable one. These trends will continue into the next century.

The Baby Boomers

All long-term trends are marked by periodic deviations. The so-called "Baby Boom" created a youth wave in the middle of the 20th century and will magnify the proportion of elderly in the early part of the next century. Population experts trace the Baby Boom to the end of the Second World War, when returning GIs entered the labor force and founded families with vigor. It was a time of incredible optimism and expansion in both human and economic terms. This period of high birth rates, begun in 1946, continued until roughly 1964, when it is said the invention of birth control pills allowed folks to put a brake on their reproductive potential. Economic downturns and a more pessimistic outlook in subsequent decades help to explain why parents have chosen to bring fewer children into the world since then.

Even though the Baby Boom lasted less than two decades, those born during that period constitute roughly a third of the total U.S. population in the late nineties. Compared to the rest of the population, their collective life journey has been likened to a pig slowly inching through the digestive canal of a python, successively challenging all social and economic institutions along the way. At first, there was a crunch at hospital maternity wards, and then schools, colleges, the job market, and housing felt the pressure. Their dominating influence shaped the youth and "yuppie" cultures. The first Boomers reached age 50, or mid-life, in 1996. They will soon command the aging agenda as they prepare for retirement in 2010 through 2030.

Even though the Boomers grew up in a period of relative peace and prosperity, their sheer numbers created fierce competition in education and the job market, while driving up real estate prices once they reached nesting age. By the same token, once Boomers had passed through stages of the life cycle, shortages turned into surpluses. The collapse of the real estate market in the late eighties is a case in point. Now, looking to the future, we can expect rising demand for retirement housing, elder care and, finally, the funeral industry, as the Boomers take leave of this world in the 2030s.

While 40-ish Boomers currently hold the center stage in terms of wealth and social and political power, the successor generations need to be considered as well. Folks in their 20s have been labeled "Baby Busters" and "Generation X." These Baby Boom offspring face both advantages and hardships in the future. On the one hand, competition in the educational system is not quite so stiff; on the other hand, they will be hard pressed, collectively, to pay for the retirement benefits of the immense Boomer generation which preceded them. This issue of "dependency," which links the generations, will be discussed in a later chapter. Suffice it to say here that some analysts predict a generational war over this issue early in the 21st century.

Using information which is currently available, forecasters have been able to create a fairly good picture of what the elderly Boomers will be like. Some of this may surprise you. The definition of "old age" will have changed. Sixty-five years constituted the average male life span during the 30s and was arbitrarily chosen as the moment when a person became classified as elderly. It marked a person's exit from the work force and signaled eligibility for pensions, Social Security, tax relief, etc. While the magic number 65 still exists, life spans have increased and will continue to do so. Currently, the "old-old," those over 85, are growing at a rapid pace, and centenarians are no longer rarities. The Census Bureau estimates that America will have approximately 100,000 individuals aged 100 and above by the year 2000, with a massive expansion of this age group in the decades to follow. (See Figure 2.) Medical specialists

Figure 2

Projections of the U.S. Population Age 100 Years and Older: 1990 – 2050

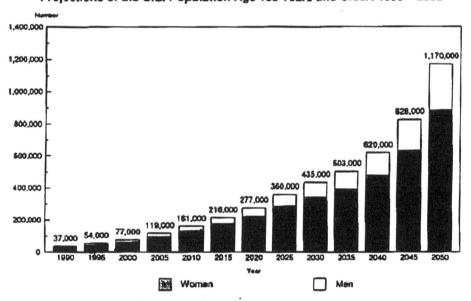

Source: U.S. Bureau of the Census, *Current Population Reports*, P25-1092

The Art of Forecasting

on aging estimate that normal human life spans may well reach into the one-hundred-teens in the next century. More about this in the Health Care Chapters.

The number of elderly in American society has been doubling every thirty years since 1900. In 1990 there were 20 elders for every 100 working-age adults; in 2025 the proportion of elderly will rise to 32 per 100. Ultimately, the baby boomers will depart, and the percentage of young people will rise by the middle of the next century. There was some speculation that the Boomers' children would repeat the cycle, but the "echo" phenomenon is very faint. In the long term, demographers predict that people will be distributed almost equally across the age spectrum (see Figure 3).

Of course, numbers don't tell the whole story. For one thing, the entire future population, including the elderly, will be much more diverse than their counterparts of today. We've always thought of America as a country dominated by people from North European stock, with a smattering of other races. While African-Americans constituted the largest minority group for most of our history, Hispanic and Asian immigrants are now quickly catching up. Considering their higher birth rates, the Census Bureau calculates that non-Hispanic Whites, today's majority, will constitute only half of the country's population by 2050. It has already happened in Hawaii and New Mexico, where no single group is the majority. California, our most populous state, will be in the same situation around the year 2000. Visit Miami, San Francisco, or San Antonio to get an impression of our population in the next century. Since the relation between ethnicity and socioeconomic status still persists, a disproportionate number of well-to-do elder whites will be juxtaposed with a growing number of relatively deprived young Hispanics and African Americans in the next century. The more pessimistic forecasters see the seeds of social conflict in this equation.

Figure 3

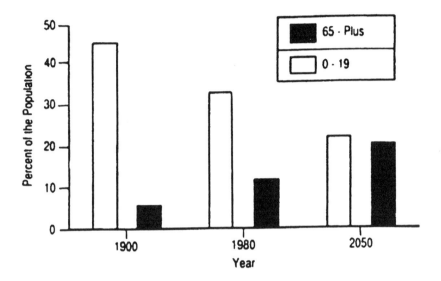

Actual and Projected
Change in Distribution of Children
and 65+ Persons in the Population,
1900–2050 (*Source:* U.S. Bureau of the
Census, *Current Population Reports*, Series
P-25, No. 952; and Census of the Population,
1900.)

The future elderly also challenge other preconceptions we may have. It is true that people become increasingly frail and require care as the years advance. Yet, current evidence proves that physical decline can be delayed, and we can enjoy robust health and lead rich, fulfilling lives long beyond the dictates of conventional wisdom. Dr. Charles Longino, a noted gerontologist, exposed "Myths of Aging" by citing the Baby Boomers' healthier lifestyles: Falling rates of cigarette smoking, reduced fat diets, exercise programs, and environmental awareness have already cut into disease and disability rates. Compared to those before them, the next generation of elderly will not only be healthier, but also much better educated and informed. When combined with their numbers, this capacity will give them unprecedented organizational and political clout to advance their agenda. Recent events in Florida politics offer an instructive leading indicator: Elder power has slowed spending programs for children, while a new state agency was created to represent the needs and concerns of older citizens.

II. Technology Innovation: The Ordeal of Change

Rummaging through my attic recently, I came upon a deteriorating stack of *Modern Mechanix* magazines from the mid-40s. Among construction plans for sanitary dog houses and dish-drying racks were articles describing the technical marvels of the next 50 years. Some ideas, like the automated car wash, have indeed been realized; on the other hand, we have not discarded our cars to commute in personal helicopters and planes. Most speculation about future technology, unfortunately, has been limited to exotic cars, planes, and household gadgets worthy of the Jetsons.

Genuine technological change takes place in a more profound way. Scholars more or less agree that human civilization has passed through a relatively small number of truly fundamental technological changes. The first was man's transition from a life of nomadic hunting and gathering to agriculture between 8,000 and 10,000 years ago. The second was the industrial age, launched by the mechanical inventions in Europe between the 17th and 18th centuries. The third transformation is happening right now with the advent of the "information age," based largely on the unexpected invention of computers. Figure 4 charts the pace of these developments. Daniel Bell, the renowned scholar, described the current phenomenon as the "Post-Industrial" society Alvin and Heidi Toffler's 1980 best seller, *The Third Wave*, while analyzed the historical consequences and noted the breathtaking changes our future will experience from digital technology.

There are, of course, a bewildering array of other technological wonders in the world today. These range from advances in genetic engineering to synthetic foods and energy from renewable sources. Some of them will be discussed in later chapters. Nevertheless, computer and information technology is the most profound agent of change, and has outpaced all others in order of importance.

What makes computers so special? To begin with, this technology is a powerful catalyst, advancing and transforming other technologies. Some applications, such as astronavigation and human gene mapping, are beyond the comprehension of the average person; on the other hand, the internet and bar code check-out at the supermarket are becoming downright pedestrian. If you recently bought a computer, you know how quickly new developments made your precious purchase obsolete. Forecasters predict that this trend will accelerate in the next decades, as enhanced computers and related communication gear challenge the human mind and transform our society.

From a purely economic perspective, the information age promises to be as revolutionary as the industrial revolution and the rise of mass production two centuries ago. At that time, highly efficient machines replaced hordes of manual laborers and individual craftsmen. The machine age is now reaching its logical conclusion in robotic factories, which need only a

Figure 4

Waves of Technology Innovation

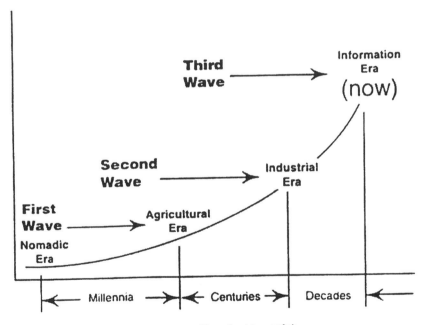

Time (not to scale)

handful of workers to monitor the assembly lines. The next generation of digital technology is capable of performing "white collar" tasks, such as accounting and mechanical drafting. This is happening right now. Later generations will make serious inroads into the technical and professional fields. Robot surgery has already been performed, and many other professionals, like educators, will find themselves replaced by screens and keyboards. If the present is an accurate guide to the future, the potential for technological progress in the next century is truly mind boggling.

The post-industrial age clearly has the potential to make human life better by enhancing useful technologies and boosting economic productivity. So what is the problem? Whenever profound technological advances occur, individuals and society must also adapt to changed circumstances. Each economic system creates a stable social order which, when disrupted, results in turmoil and anxiety for displaced individuals. To put it into perspective, the impact of the information revolution may well be as profound as the social changes which took place when farmers migrated to industrial cities. What a shock to leave the "Little House on the Prairie," and become a time-clock-punching grease monkey on the Detroit assembly line! Now it's our turn.

The down side of increased digital technology is its effect on employment. Like all new economic systems, a distinct set of workers, values, and social organizations are required. Historically, the trend has been toward fewer and fewer workers; in our era, the digital revolution may well finish the job! Suffice it to say here that the concept of work will take on a new meaning in the next century. Fewer workers will be needed, and those who have jobs will perform tasks which, for various reasons, cannot be performed by smart machines. Later chapters will explore the consequences more fully.

It promises to be a heady time for those who own or operate chunks of the information economy. Many others, unfortunately, will experience frustration as the booming digital economy makes their industrial-age skills obsolete. With education and training, some brainy, ambitious folks will be able to mount the "Third Wave" and ride it. The rest face an uncertain future. Which way are you headed?

III. Economic Prospects of the Post-Industrial Society

America is a wealthy, powerful country and will no doubt remain so for a number of centuries. We have ample natural resources, bountiful arable land, high levels of technology, and a dynamic population. Nevertheless, our economy has been slowing down. During the frontier period of the 1800s, economic growth rates, measured in GNP, exceeded 10 percent annually. Current rates hover around two percent, and only the most optimistic economists predict a return to the heady four percent rates of the booming 1960s. In all fairness, eventual economic slowdown is a common feature of all mature industrial societies, where diminishing returns in productivity and saturation of capacities have taken place. Eventually the booming economies in the newly-industrialized Pacific rim countries must follow the same pattern.

Looking ahead, economic forecasters consider the interaction of several key factors which will shape our economy in the next century. One of these is the burden of personal and public debt accumulated in the latter half of the 20th century. Future obligations, particularly society's responsibility to support elder care entitlements for numerous Baby Boomers, figure prominently here. Then there is the matter of lagging investments, which predisposes future productivity. International economic forces are also gaining in importance. And finally, we need to consider the future economic implications of the information revolution. Let's take a closer look.

Will Debt be a Problem?

What dirty little secret is shared by an increasing number of our relatives, friends, and neighbors? You guessed it: maxed-out credit cards and the prospect of dates with the bankruptcy court (see Figure 5). Although folks have had credit problems since the invention of money, the current era is witnessing unprecedented levels of default. While it's easy to scold individuals for overspending, remember that the corporate world and our government share the same basic problem. Why?

While mainstream economists predict declining future growth, our historical tradition still assumes that each generation will be more prosperous than its predecessors. A common theme in American family histories seems to be how the struggle and sacrifices of grandparents culminated in the prosperity of their descendants. This is the essence of the "American Dream." So how can we cope with the prospects of a less abundant future? In recent years, the answer was borrowing money to satisfy material expectations. Credit, after all, had made sense in an expanding economy when the means for repayment were just around the corner. Individuals, corporations, and government operated under this philosophy.

The really big credit binge began sometime in the late 60s and early 70s. Banks and credit card issuers learned that they could earn phenomenal profits on interest charges of unpaid balances, goading the consumers to max out their credit line. The frightening increase in consumer debt is a familiar tale and need not be retold here. In the same way, the corporate merger and acquisition frenzy of the 80s was financed with borrowed money; the melt-down of the savings and loan industry turned out to be one of the most frightening examples of reckless borrowing and speculation in the annals of business history. Finally, there is government, the ultimate lender and borrower in our society. Its problem has not differed much from that of the consumer piling up credit card debt. We, the citizens, have a voracious appetite for government benefits and services,

Figure 5

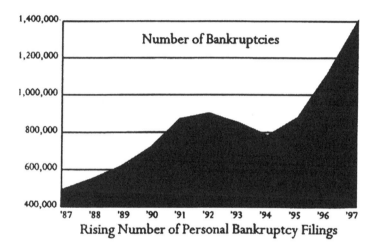

Number of Bankruptcies

Rising Number of Personal Bankruptcy Filings

Source: U.S. Department of Commerce

but are reluctant to pay the necessary taxes. Deficit spending has been the solution.

We now have budget deficits, which represent government's annual shortfall, plus a national debt, the sum of accumulated deficits. The deficit is measured in the billions and the debt in trillions, something like four trillion in the late 90s. Figure 6 traces the growth of our national obligations. (And remember that state and local governments are rarely debt free). While the principal is staggering, annual interest obligations are sobering enough. In the late 90s, the annual interest bill hovered around $200 billion a year, representing something like 15 percent of the federal budget. Symbolic gestures, like amending the Constitution, will not balance the budget and make the problem go away. So what are the prospects for slaying this deficit dragon?

Until the late 90s, the last balanced budget occurred in the mid-60s. Since then, the "spending opportunities" have far outnumbered any savings. The Vietnam War cost plenty; then came some of the most generous social entitlement programs in our history. Spending our way to prosperity with "Supply Side" economics tripled the national debt in the 1980s. This was followed by the savings and loan bailout. Future scenarios include a multi-billion dollar cleanup of the nuclear industry and federal aid to a faltering pension guarantee system. Worst of all, the true size of the federal deficits is masked by huge Social Security surplus deposits, which is owed to retirees in the 21st century. This particular problem will be discussed in the third chapter.

Obviously, credit and government deficits are not viable answers to a prosperous future. So what avenues can we create? There are both optimistic and pessimistic scenarios. The optimists, many of whom make their homes in Washington, believe that America can grow out of debt. They suppose that slightly higher rates of growth and a little more fiscal discipline will, over time, shrink the debt in proportion to the general economy. The pessimistic scenario, forecast by many conservative economists, projects declining growth rates, further debt accumulation, and some eventual crisis. The old saying that we owe the national debt only to ourselves is not completely true. Many foreigners have also invested in traditionally stable U.S. government securities. Could we pay back all creditors if a crisis destroyed their faith in our financial health? The darkest, though least probable, scenario would involve repudiation of debts, as Latin American countries attempted in the 80s, and more printing of money to wash out the obligations in a wave of hyperinflation, as Germany did in the 20s.

Lagging Investment

Mainstream economists agree that a lack of investment counts among the greatest problems associated with excessive indebtedness. Simply put, investment means saving part of one's current income to make productive improvements which result in greater future gains or benefits. At the individual level, this might be job training, while industry might invest in new plants or machinery. It's a worthwhile sacrifice for the sake of future productivity.

Government sector investment means "infrastructure" improvements, typically repairs to utilities, roads, bridges, and public facilities. Sadly enough, savings, which are the normal source of investments, dry up during periods of personal, corporate and public deficits. In other words, the money is needed for debt service. This trend jeopardizes our future prosperity. While lack of investment clouds the future of many U.S. industries, economists predict that high rates of savings and investment in some other countries will pay off handsomely in terms of their future productivity.

Meanwhile, we also have neglected investment in the public realm. Deteriorating roads and bridges are most visible, but the real future crisis may be in terms of human investment.

Total Federal Debt

(Trillions of Dollars)

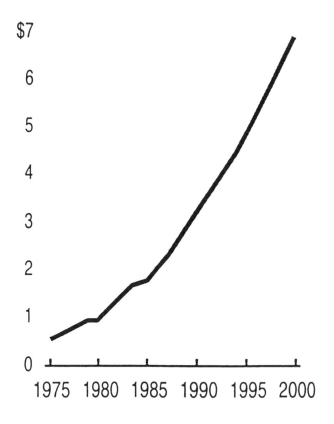

Source: 1975 – 1995: Budget of the U.S.
        Government, FY 1996; 1996 – 2000
        Congressional Budget Office Projections

Figure 6

Far too many people are not getting the knowledge and skills needed to become productive participants in the predicted post-industrial society of the 21st century. Worse yet are the increasing proportions of deprived children growing up in the nation's urban and rural slums. Government statistics from the 90s concluded that one out of five American children lived below the official poverty level; in some communities the proportion has been much higher. Handicapped by inadequate nutrition, health care, adult supervision, and education, these youngsters are growing up to become a burden rather than an asset to society. It is surely in our best interest to see that adequate human investments are made here!

Globalization

Although trade among nations has existed since ancient times, we are only now witnessing a true "globalization" of our economy. By opening their doors, free trade countries like America gain access to the best and most reasonably priced raw materials and manufactured goods other nations have to offer. This benefits us as consumers; few other countries provide the public with such a rich offering of merchandise at extremely reasonable prices. If you think our prices are high, try shopping in Japan, Europe, or other regions that don't practice free trade.

On the other hand, free trade creates hazards for U.S. workers and manufacturers as they compete with foreign labor. If other countries also practice free trade, superior and reasonably-priced American products can be successfully sold overseas. This translates into American jobs and economic well being, a best case scenario. Unfortunately, many other countries erect barriers against U.S. imports, in which case our manufacturers compete against foreigners only at home. This stunts American production and employment. For example, the much-improved and reasonably-priced new American cars face a hostile market overseas. There is no question that foreign trade has a significant effect on this country's economic system.

Continuing improvements in communication and transportation technology will accelerate economic globalization. Not only ship and air transport, but pipelines, satellites, and electronic links now connect the world's economic systems. Interdependence among trading partners is unavoidable. For instance, our economy depends on cheap petroleum from the Middle East; any political crisis in that region might disrupt the oil flow and create ripple effects throughout our economy. Likewise, our free trade pact with Mexico had chilling consequences for low-skilled American workers. International trade is a complex subject. Suffice it to say that as globalization continues, our lives will be profoundly impacted by what happens in faraway lands. More about this in later chapters.

The Political Agenda of the Next Century

While the foregoing forecasts are rooted in well-documented past and present developments, government policy is somewhat of a "wild card," twisting in the shifting political winds of the moment. Like everything else, we can be certain that the members of the Baby Boom generation will determine the agenda for the next several decades. Paul Light, author of *Baby Boomers*, claims that this generation is hard to define politically, since boomers sport both liberal and conservative views. Here's a sample: Most are fiscal conservatives and denounce expanding government's role. Boomers also favor an "opportunity society" which maximizes personal freedom and space, while observing tolerance for other people's values and lifestyles. On the other hand, members of this generation are also very security conscious. They are concerned about crime, the environment, and, most of all, the future security of government entitlement programs like Social Security and Medicare. If this sounds a little contradictory, it is.

In terms of domestic politics, the single hot issue will be

future entitlements for the elderly. Figure 7 illustrates the trend. We already know that in future decades the number of senior citizens and their needs will be greatly magnified. We also know that economic austerity lies ahead. What happens when these two trends meet in the political arena? Some astute forecasters warn that a clash between working and retired generations cannot be avoided. Those who reach retirement age in the latter part of the 2Oth century, for the most part, enjoy a far more comfortable existence than prior generations of elderly. Increased Social Security benefits, Medicare, tax relief, and a host of other government programs have helped them fend off destitution in their sunset years. Pockets of deprivation remain, typically among minorities and elderly women, but programs like Supplementary Security Income and Medicaid provid a safety net.

Government benefit programs for the elderly have always occupied the moral high ground. According to opinion surveys, most Americans think of the elderly as deserving; poverty in old age is commonly linked to sacrifices and inequities in earlier years. Furthermore, senior citizen entitlements also enjoy the support of vocal and well-organized interest groups. The American Association of Retired Persons (AARP) is one of the largest membership groups in America and richly deserves its title of "King Kong" of the lobbying groups in Washington. Can you imagine the AARP's influence as more and more Baby Boomers hit the membership roles?

While many Boomers expect the same, and even expanded benefits on their retirement, a few brave souls have warned that this is neither realistic nor desirable in the context of future economic and demographic projections. This backlash can be traced to a group of journalists, academics, and political figures who united under the banner of **Americans For Intergenerational Equity** in the mid-80s. Calling themselves a "Lobby for the Future," they argued that by continuing high

Figure 7

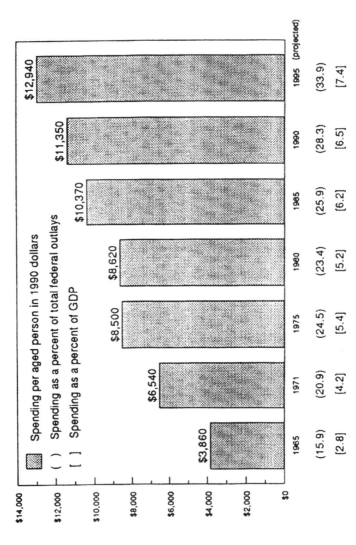

Estimated Federal Spending on Aged Persons, Fiscal Years 1965 – 1995

Spending per aged person in 1990 dollars
( ) Spending as a percent of total federal outlays
[ ] Spending as a percent of GDP

	1965	1971	1975	1980	1985	1990	1995 (projected)
Spending per aged person	$3,860	$6,540	$8,500	$8,620	$10,370	$11,350	$12,940
Percent of total federal outlays	(15.9)	(20.9)	(24.5)	(23.4)	(25.9)	(28.3)	(33.9)
Percent of GDP	[2.8]	[4.2]	[5.4]	[5.2]	[6.2]	[6.5]	[7.4]

Source: Committee on Ways and Means, U.S. House of Representatives, *Overview of Entitlement Programs, 1992 Green Book*

levels of social spending for the elderly, we would surely destroy the nation's fiscal integrity in the next century. Since then, members of Generation X, or Baby Busters, have claimed this cause as their own. Their argument is that most elder benefits are based on age criteria alone and tend to waste public funds where need may not exist. Why, for instance, should a retired millionaire receive free medical care, or a 68-year-old pay less taxes than a 30-year-old with the same income? Need, rather than age, should dictate who gets the break. At the same time, we should resist "fiscal child abuse. We need to invest more heavily in the needs of deprived children who will not become productive adults without active intervention.

The best possible resolution of this issue might be some intergenerational compact in which different age groups acknowledge their mutual dependence. Prosperous, self-sufficient senior citizens are less of a burden to young family members, while healthy, well-educated youngsters have a greater capacity to help support older relatives in need. This mutually-supportive family analogy should be applied to society as a whole.

Likely Solutions

Government is everyone's favorite whipping boy. Yet, we know full well that our elected officials do respond to the people who elected them. The problem, perhaps, is that different groups in society pull in different directions, while the Constitution's system of checks and balances tends to resist changes which do not have the support of overwhelming majorities over time. "Democracy is a political system where angels elect devils," goes the old French proverb. In fact, our representatives survive in public office by avoiding hard choices and providing constituents with generous benefits while avoiding the bane of taxation, which constitutes political suicide. This is why Social Security has been called the "Third Rail" of American politics; touch it and you're dead.

Nevertheless, the problem will not go away but becomes more intense as society's bills come due. The political mood of the 90s has been very nostalgic. Rather than dealing with problems of the present and future, Americans sought an escape to the past, when government was smaller and people took care of themselves. Many of us long for the serene, small-town America depicted by Norman Rockwell, and secretly wish that millions of urban slum-dwellers might somehow be transformed into the Waltons, living simple, virtuous, and self-sufficient lives in their bucolic rural paradise. But that is not to be. The virtues rooted in the social and economic systems of earlier epochs cannot be resurrected. Moreover, we tend to forget the dark side of our historical experience. Serious historians point out that life in early America was not always a picnic but marked by plenty of violence, injustice, and poverty. Colonial times were extremely harsh for ordinary people, and even the much-idealized 1950s had more than a few dark spots. No, we can't turn back the clocks.

The ultimate and inevitable direction of future policies will follow the typical way our government has always operated. That is, playing for time until a true crisis or disaster appears inevitable. Politicians call this the "train wreck" scenario. At that point, compromises are made to save essential elements of the system. Implementation is typically stretched over a long time so that citizens will not be alarmed. In the case of elder entitlement programs, like Medicare and Social Security, the second and third decades of the next century will witness a gradual phase-out of most benefits for prosperous retirees, while maintaining a safety net for those who would be destitute without it. Chapter 3 tells how all of this will affect you.

Chapter 2

YOUR WORK AND CAREER: A Tale of Hazards and Opportunities

Imagine the world as a garden where happy people play, while somewhere, out of sight, mindless robots do all the work. This liberating vision, promoted by many utopian futurists, is only half true. Yes, automation is indeed taking over many human tasks, but for most folks the world is not turning into a garden of delights. Displaced veterans of the industrial age face the chilling reality of unemployment and declining wages. Meanwhile, those clever or fortunate few, who have made the successful leap into the post-industrial information age, may reasonably expect to live happily ever after. The arrival of the Third Wave has enormous human consequences, and this chapter summarizes both dangers and opportunities awaiting us.

Automation: The Revolution in the Workplace

It's no secret that industrial processes are increasingly becoming automated; robots are taking over the physical tasks once performed by manual laborers. This is a logical continuation of a trend started many years ago. More recently, the second generation of computers made it possible to automate clerical tasks. Succeeding generations of computers are taking over highly-skilled and managerial tasks and futurists predict that the work of highly trained professionals in such fields as law, medicine, and engineering may become partially, if not totally, automated with the advanced computer networks, imaging technology, massive data storage, and artificial intelligence coming off the drawing boards.

Uncle Milton, who recently retired, worked his way up to manager of a hardware store. When he first started in the business, customers walked up to a store counter, and clerks brought them requested merchandise from shelves behind them or the storage room in the back. That changed with the gradual introduction of the self-service concept after the War. Except for small, valuable items, which could be easily pilfered, the merchandise became directly accessible to the shoppers. According to Milton, self-service had several advantages: It liberated the impulse buyers, it made the customers do the work of making product decisions, and required the customers to carry their purchases to the cash register. The boss also liked the fact that fewer clerks were required. Ultimately, the only remaining staff consisted of two cash register attendants, a hard-to-find stock clerk, and the manager, who watched the operations of the business from a closed-circuit TV in a cubicle. Oh yes, let's not forget about the rent-a-cop who guarded the door.

As efficient as it seemed, Milton noted that the store has recently lost much of its business to mail-order houses, which operated on a larger scale, using even fewer employee. He would be amazed to learn how few retail workers will be needed in the next century, when people have the communication technology to do nearly all of their shopping from home. It's already possible to order merchandise through the internet. For those who still order via telephone, a home bar code reading attachment will soon be available. Customers will be able to scan catalog entries and then transmit this information to a remote warehouse where an automated shipping system will fill their orders and send them out.

You don't have to look far for more examples. Do you remember the man at the gas station who washed your car with a hose, sponge, and bucket of suds? Or how about the banks, with long rows of teller windows, each manned by an attractive young woman? Both occupations are now performed by large metal boxes! Look around you and see how many other manual and clerical occupations have been replaced by machines. Now, imagine what will happen as the pace accelerates.

While many occupations will become obsolete, others will be dramatically altered by information technology in the next century. Forecasters envision farmers who work principally indoors. While remote-controlled robot tractors till the fields and harvest the crops, farmer Brown stays glued to his computer terminal, calculating production data, the impact of long-range weather forecasts, and optimum fertilizer use in terms of market figures supplied by the internet. Factories will be largely devoid of humans, with only a few individuals to monitor and maintain industrial robots. Meanwhile, computers are proving useful as one-on-one educational devices in the schools, while the military and law enforcement agencies are turning to robot scouts and sentinels for those situations which could place their human personnel in harm's way. These machines, by the way, won't ever complain about overtime, demand fringe benefits, or join a union. They're the ideal employees.

Is no one exempt? Skeptics like to point out that only humans can master higher intellectual processes involved in the traditional professions. There is a consensus that ultimate decisions, based on values and ethics ,should remain in the human realm. On the other hand, recent developments in artificial intelligence, like fuzzy logic, suggest that we are far from reaching the limit. It is more likely to enhance rather than replace professions. For example, robot surgery provides the doctor with a truly exact and steady hand, while a quick computer search of court records would permit a lawyer to skip much of the tedious research needed to prepare a case. To be sure, modern airliners are already so highly automated that, except for takeoffs and landings, the pilots are little more than observant passengers.

Human Consequences of the Information Revolution

As automation of industrial and clerical operations proceeds, job opportunities are increasingly concentrated in the service sector. This is because there are still no robots able to work as hair dressers, nurses, short order cooks, psychological counselors, or topless dancers. Even here, future automation is not out of the question. Since wages for most service workers are relatively low, the incentive for business to replace them is not yet here. To be sure, workers are often told that meager salaries are absolutely necessary to protects their jobs. Ultimately, of course, the information revolution will also make inroads in the service sector. Few occupations are exempt. The psychological counselor of the future may well be a computer; the patient responds to a list of complaints and then receives appropriate therapeutic advice on the screen. Likewise, holographic images generated by virtual reality devices may outperform any human entertainer. Computer technicians on the fringe are said to be developing virtual cyber sex devices. Connected through the internet, an individual wearing a touch screen leotard would interact with an analogous humanoid robot manipulated by an equally-equipped romantic partner at some other location. From an occupational standpoint, legal and hygienic prostitution may be at hand!

Historians note that any great technological revolution has wrenching human consequences. We are now entering such a period. It began in the 70s, when the introduction of smart machines laid off industrial assembly line workers. Then, a vast increase in economic globalization accelerated the process of de-industrialization in our country. International trade is a great idea; it permits countries to specialize in what they do best. In addition, world scale competition provides consumers with the best possible products at the lowest prices. Unfortunately, some other countries hold a competitive advantage in terms of industrial labor costs, bad news for America's workers. Finally, more stringent environmental regulations, which have done so much for our health, forced smokestack industries to concentrate in regions with less stringent pollution laws. In this era of disappearing factory jobs, some industrial workers have been able to move up with information age skills; most, however, find themselves settling for low-wage jobs in retail, food service, or other branches of the service sector.

Yuppies? Fire When Ready!

At the dawn of the information revolution, smug, college-educated technical and managerial people enjoyed the benefits of Japanese cars, French wines, and other imported goodies in a healthier, natural environment. These Yuppies, (Young Urban Professional People), believed that their jobs would be safe from both foreign competition and automation. How wrong they were! The 80s and 90s witnessed a tidal wave of corporate acquisitions, mergers, restructuring, and downsizing. Figure 1 summarizes major corporate cuts taken in the early 90s. All companies had the same goal: Use economies of scale supported by information age technologies to eliminate large segments of the high-salary, white-collar work force. IBM, for instance, reduced its work force by half from the late 80s to the early 90s. The long-range impact on mid-life Baby Boomers, and their

Downsizing

COMPANY	DATE	LAYOFFS
AT&T	Jan. 1996	40,000
Boeing	Feb. 1993	28,000
Chemical/Chase Manhattan	Aug. 1995	12,000
Delta Air Lines	Apr. 1994	15,000
Digital Equipment	May 1994	20,000
General Motors	Dec. 1991	74,000
GTE Corp.	Jan. 1994	17,000
IBM	July 1993	60,000
McDonnell Douglas	July 1990	17,000
NYNEX	Jan. 1994	16,800
Philip Morris	Nov. 1993	14,000
Sears, Roebuck & Co.	Jan. 1993	50,000
Scott Paper	N/A	11,000

Source: *Newsweek*, February 26, 1996

retirement prospects will be discussed in the next chapter. Trimming middle management had the desired result of reducing costs and increasing corporate profitability. While the downsized employees were less than happy, financial markets greeted the news with glee. From all indications, this basic trend will continue well into the 21st century, as successive generations of Third Wave technologies liberate workers from physical and mental tasks. Who knows, Yuppies may turn into Yuffies, Young Urban Failures.

While the corporate giants are shedding personnel, there has been a remarkable growth of smaller companies. You might ask why. Out-sourcing and subcontracting has a lot to do with it. Instead of performing all operations in-house, many businesses subcontract their work to smaller companies with lower overhead and labor costs. This is often accomplished by a temporary work force. Everyone is doing it. In the case of government, various tasks, such as prisons, are being privatized, while colleges and universities increasingly use lower-paid, part-time faculty. Start-up companies typically don't have to contend with entrenched unions, benefit plans, and other burdens of established enterprises; nor do they have to maintain a brand name-image or reputation. The after-market of Brand X auto parts is a great example. Finally, it is not uncommon for downsized, corporate workers to find themselves performing identical tasks with a no name firm which sprang up to become a supplier to their old employer.

Ultimately, more and more large businesses are destined to become virtual enterprises, which means that, except for a small headquarters cadre, all operations will be performed by others. The sportswear manufacturer Nike is a precursor. Multimillion dollar advertising campaigns would lead you to think that these are American products. Not so. There is no Nike factory; shoes, shirts, and all other merchandise is produced by a legion of third world contractors who follow manufacturing standards dictated from the home office. As you can imagine, the combination of an American image with third world labor costs yields astounding profits.

Of course, the virtual business mode can also be beneficial for us. Forecasters point to a future where creative people use information technologies to mold individual careers. Already, many professionals are telecommuting, working out of their own homes, connected to the world through personal computers and modems. Many tasks, such as consulting, literary editing, or stock market analysis, require neither a city office, nor face-to-face contact with a boss. Some imaginative folks can be expected to move from the virtual office into virtual enterprises, which will cater to the unique needs of the dispersed information age economy.

A Visit to the 21st Century Workplace

While we're at it, let's take a look at this workplace of the future. During the machine age, workers went to their jobs. Now, the information age brings tasks to people wherever they are. It probably started when sales people and managers of far-flung enterprises started hitting the road. You gave up your office for a company car and a lap-top computer. Then, cellular telephones allowed you to conduct business while driving or scurrying through airports. Considering advances in data-transmission, the trend is likely to continue.

But wait, the resulting freedom may be an illusion. Having electronic access to everyone imaginable is great, until you realize that they will also have continuous and instantaneous access to you! Until recently, only doctors had beepers to alert them of critical emergencies. Now, everyone seems to be on call; privacy and free time get lost in the process. Psychologists warn about rising levels of stress and anxiety as people are subjected to the techno-hell of unfettered work-place crises while on vacation or enjoying quality time with loved ones.

Tired of lugging your lap-top around? Futurists predict that the next generation of personal computers will be worn as an integral part of your clothing. Paradoxically, top executives in the future organizational hierarchy may be rewarded with reduced, rather than expanded, communication gear! By the way, paperwork will continue to pile up. At one time, futurists had predicted the paperless office. It turns out that people continue to insist on hard copy, making the paperless office about as likely as the paperless bathroom.

Finally, there's a dehumanizing side to the virtual office. Despite the availability of so much communication technology, managers should consider the potential for frustration and isolation on the part of individual workers or clients. There's always a gap between the human mind and our information technology. Currently, the latter is exploding at such a rate that many folks become paralyzed from information overload and lose their creative instincts. Consider voice mail and other modern telephone devices which save labor by eliminating a human response at the end of the line. You want to call someone and get something done. Instead, a computer-generated recording at the other end instructs you to enter a bewildering series of numbers and codes on your keyboard without, of course, connecting you to the party you have in mind. The truth is that these devices are largely designed to prevent rather than facilitate communication. If you don't believe me, try calling for customer assistance the next time a computer or other piece of office machinery misbehaves. Yes, the future would be great if all technologies were easy to operate or functioned flawlessly. In fact, we are still a long way from fail-safe technologies, and for most folks the frustrating consequences of equipment breakdown are only a mouse-click away.

Finally, there's no hard data on what will happen when the virtual workplace eliminates the human contact within organizations. Opinion surveys reveal that personal relations counted among the most positive aspects of individuals' work experience. Indeed, social psychologists suggest that frequent human interactions help bond organizations through friendly competition, mutual support, and other forms of interpersonal relations. It is unlikely that electronic substitutes like teleconferencing will create the loyalty and cooperative spirit which are the hallmarks of successful enterprises.

Can we Learn from Corporate Reorganization?

Perhaps we can apply some lessons of corporate restructuring to our personal lives and career plans. Personnel management policies of the past several decades were not so much a diabolical plot to harass and uproot employees as they were a way of staying competitive during the transition from the mass production to the service-based technology and information-driven economy. The former was orderly and predictable, the latter flexible and subject to global forces as it evolved. Just as corporations restructure themselves to survive the challenges of this environment, individuals must do the same. Mass production required order and stability, putting golden handcuffs on suitable employees. Now, employees must shed the cookie cutter mentality of the assembly line and rethink their career plans in terms of individual differences and advantages which make them unique. Career development, from this perspective, becomes an adventure with both risks and opportunities. The easy ride may be over.

So, what will happen to those who are not so lucky? The politically correct answer is that everyone should become computer literate, either early or later, and jump on the information age bandwagon. However, opportunities will be limited by large numbers of middle-aged, former middle-income people needing employment. Some will be forced out of the work force altogether, while others scramble for remaining service sector jobs. It will be harder to make ends meet, especially for those released from middle management jobs. The decline of real wages, which began in the 70s, promises to be more than just dry Labor Department statistics for many folks. When a politician boasted of having created millions of new jobs in the mid-90s, a weary citizen replied, Yes, and I hold three of them."

The End of Work

Our current anxiety about jobs and job security is real. Scholars such as Thomas Moore, in his 1996 book, *The Disposable Work Force,* make no bones about it. The controversial but ever prescient futurist Jeremy Rifkin got to the heart of the problem when he published *The End of Work* in 1996. Rifkin's thesis, pure and simple, is that fewer and fewer workers will be needed to provide society with necessary goods and services in the future. Unfortunately, this may not yield a utopia of leisure and prosperity for all. It is more likely to cause severe social problems in the 21st century. Since biblical times, a person's worth has been calculated in terms of mental and physical labor. It gives our lives purpose and meaning. Traditional jobs will be scarce in the next century. Some folks may have temporary or part-time jobs, while large numbers can expect to be unemployable on a permanent basis.

Americans probably cannot follow those Europeans who are moving toward dividing available jobs among workers by granting longer vacations and shorter work weeks. This flexible, underemployment approach is hardly compatible with America's traditional work ethic, which considers the 40-hour week and two-week vacation as established by God. Furthermore, a communal approach to work might sever the traditional link between individual productivity and pay.

The prospect of mass unemployment presents totally new problems to both individuals and society. Individuals will need to have satisfying and constructive activities to occupy their projected longer life spans. All of us know the potential for crime and anti-social behavior if people are left to their own devices. Likewise, income and income distribution will be a serious problem in a future world without work. Our economic system distributes wages according to the scale of contributions to productivity; what will happen if only a handfull of people who own and operate the economy are the productive ones? Surely some ways will have to be found to support the rest. It promises to be especially difficult as long as the work ethic remains enshrined as the principal virtue in our society. The most chilling forecasts envision some futuristic class conflict between haves and have-nots. Let's hope that future generations will have the wisdom to accommodate changing realities and values in a humane fashion.

Learning to Learn: Flexible Education for the 21st Century

One way of dealing with these bewildering prospects is to rethink the process of education. Before this can happen, some of today's conventional wisdom must be discarded. For instance, we can no longer think of the occupational world as a pegboard where each hole represents a well-defined job or specialty. In this model the function of schools and colleges was to assure that their students, the pegs, received the qualifications to fit precisely into the slots. The notion that a career is of lifetime duration is also becoming obsolete. Simply stated, the occupational world is changing so rapidly that students must prepare themselves for frequent and unexpected moves in their professional careers.

So, how do you prepare for this uncertain future? Instead of specializing at an early age, students will receive an education that will strengthen their intellectual development and learning capacity over a lifetime. Being aware of and receptive to change will be the broader goal. Everyone agrees on the importance of computer literacy and need to work effectively with evolving technologies. Professional educators also emphasize the importance of developing creativity, social skills, and effective communication. Social skills are necessary for teamwork, customer service, and survival in a multi-cultural America. Furthermore, continued globalization of our economy will require people to gain a working knowledge of foreign languages, history, and social diversity. Some futurists contend young people in particular lack these human-to-human skills in part because today's youngsters spend more time interacting with machines—computers—than with people. As virtual reality advances, impressionable young people will be tempted to opt out of reality and lose themselves in the colorful fantasy world churned out by the video industry. Psychologists warn that mental agility is no substitute for the lessons we learn through human interaction.

Lifetime Learning: What You Must Do

In planning your personal future, the logical first step is to gain a vision of what lies ahead. The preceding sections did that. The next step involves examining personal goals, values, and capabilities in the context of future realities. Finally, we need to invest in ourselves to meet the challenges of the next century.

There will never be a substitute for knowledge, foresight and wisdom. Besides this book, there are many other publications and resources which offer insights into the future. The more we know, the better our choices are likely to be. We could begin with a commitment to **Lifelong Learning,** a concept which is coming into its own. The preceding section described how people once completed an education program at an early age, which prepared them for a lifetime occupation. It was a dull, but secure way of life. The arrival of the post-industrial information society created both insecurity and opportunity in terms of occupational qualifications. Each new stage of technology seemed to require an appropriately higher level of expertise. Only those who were truly nimble and flexible have been able to keep pace.

Managers of the most successful companies recognized this and instituted elaborate in-service training programs to keep employees up to speed. The best companies, you should realize, also have the best training programs. The process begins when a new employee arrives and continues through all stages of that individual's career. While training takes time and effort away from productive activities, the investment in a better-qualified work force pays off in the long run.

Meanwhile, the phenomenon of lifelong learning is also transforming the education industry. Until recently, colleges, universities, and other institutions of higher learning concentrated all of their energy on the education of young people. Until recently, education ended at age 22 for most folks. Now, information age skill requirements, coupled with an aging population, promise to make school a place for old-timers as well as kids. Do you remember the concept of working your way through college? Well, from now on, ambitious folks will be colleging their way through work! Educational leaders themselves will need to become futurists of the first order.

And now, a word of caution. Not all employers will have the vision to assure their workers' continued education and training. Many more are likely to take a short-term view by hiring and discarding workers as the moment demands. This is why part-time and temporary workers constituted the fastest growing segment of the work force in the 90s. Hiring people under these terms not only gives managers flexibility, but also allows them to dodge various benefits and privileges normally accrued by senior members of the work force. Under these conditions, individuals must take control of their own fate by mapping out personal training and education plans. It demands flexibility and willingness to make a serious investment in terms of time and money. But dollar for dollar, and minute for minute, it remains the single best investment you can make for the 21st century.

Job and Career Choices for the Next Century

The following is not intended to take the place of competent career counseling. Much depends on individual capabilities and preferences. Still, any career choice or change should involve consideration of the major trends discussed in the last chapter. For instance, the needs of the Baby Boomers, as they pass through various life stages, will successively invigorate and then snuff out major industries and services. No doubt, nursing and other forms of elder care will constitute major occupational groups in the 2020s. At the same time, we need to be aware of trends in technology innovation; they have a nasty way of making various jobs obsolete. Do you remember the ice man, the service station attendant, and local telephone operator? Finally, American workers must look at themselves in the international context: How well will you compete with others in the global economy?

College-trained professionals with leadership positions in the information society are now emerging as the most prosperous group in the country. Dual-income couples in this category do even better. At the opposite end are single females rearing children but without formal education or technical skills. They and their offspring are condemned to a life of low wages and misery. No surprises, right? Predictions for the rest are more interesting. Kenneth Gray and Edwin Herr noted in their 1995 book *Other Ways to Win: Creating Alternatives for High School Graduates* that many college graduates, particularly those from the liberal arts, will never be as affluent as those with technical skills. They will be in oversupply during the next century and may be turned away from various menial service positions as overqualified. The prospects are much better for high school or technical school graduates who have mastered a variety of useful up-to-date skills. Restaurant chefs, dental hygienists, criminal corrections officers, and plumbers might fall into this category. Certain tasks are simply not amenable to automation and will offer lucrative rewards to those with the requisite skills and abilities. Future society may even attach special value to human handiwork and the personal touch! Figure 2 summarizes the Labor Department's forecast of the job market in the near future.

The most painful choices, no doubt, will be made by those who have been laid off in the wake of technological advances and corporate downsizing. From a front office perspective, middle managers are the most lucrative target. Not only are their skills obsolete, but they can often be replaced by younger, lower-wage individuals. Finally, these older employees are usually entitled to costly fringe benefits and generated health care and pension costs for the company. While firing them might be a great savings opportunity for the company, the personal costs for the individuals are truly devastating. There is ample evidence that this trend, now in full swing, will continue well into the next century.

Do you know anyone in this bind? Among my acquaintances, two middle-aged individuals stand out. One is Alice, who recently lost her job as executive secretary at a TV station. It seems that after the boss got a computer, and learned word processing, Alice and her knowledge of typing and shorthand were no longer indispensable. At the same time, introduction of voice mail eliminated the need for someone to man the phone at all times. Then, when the firm's profitability dropped behind competitors, management decided to trim the fat, which meant a pink slip for Alice and several others at the station.

Then there is Richard, who had built a solid career as store manager for a supermarket chain. Richard, and others like him, had worked hard over many years to build a reputation for the store. The sparkling success of the small chain did not go unnoticed. But I'm not talking about customers; The store was noticed by corporate merger and acquisition specialists in New York. Like other successful local businesses, it became a buy-out target for a national firm. The impending merger has made many people happy: stockholders who were handsomely rewarded, and top executives of the local company who received millions to

CAREER OPPORTUNITIES

Forecast Percent Change 1994 - 2005

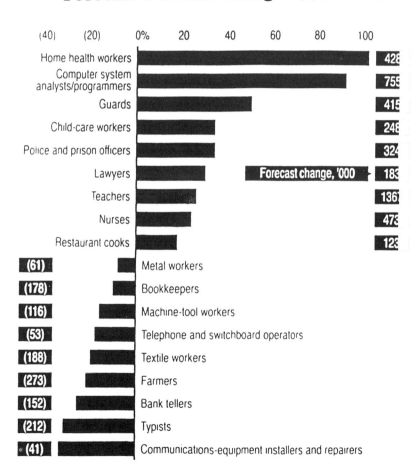

Source: U.S. Bureau of Labor Statistics, 1996; *The Economist,* September 28, 1996

assure a graceful departure. Richard is not so fortunate. The new owner offered no golden parachute to lower-level employees; rather they were encouraged to resign quietly or accept marginal jobs with the new management team responsible for revamping the stores to fit their national image. Richard was steamed, but what could he do?

Now, for the good news. Since I last spoke to them, both Alice and Richard are picking up the pieces and exploring new career paths. Richard has lined up a consulting job with a local agency which helps young entrepreneurs get started. The federal grant funding the agency will probably run out in two years, but for now Richard really enjoys what he's doing. Alice, meanwhile, is using her contacts in the broadcasting industry and her expertise with office machinery to set up a sales and distribution center for announcers' scripts. You may not know this, but much of the clever, carefree chatter from your evening news announcer or morning radio DJ is actually scripted. Thanks to her contacts, Alice has assembled a stable of writers and distributes their jokes, riddles, and funny lists to radio and TV stations. We wish her luck.

Late-life job transitions are the most difficult. Once released, an employee's lateral move to a similar position elsewhere is usually impossible. Remember how many aging Baby Boomers will find themselves in similar circumstances! The American Association of Retired People has conducted considerable research on this subject. The news is both good and bad. Despite laws which prohibit age discrimination, too many employers still harbor prejudices against older workers and try to keep them at a distance. Older workers, it is said, are slower, less flexible, and will need more sick leave and medical care. Other AARP studies indicate that these preconceptions are wrong, and that senior citizens make superior employees where judgment, reliability, experience, and honesty are important job requirements. Another trend points toward the hiring of older workers in the service sector. The good news is that barriers against older workers are falling; the bad news is that their wages may be disappointing.

As you can imagine, the business of career counseling is focusing on this phenomenon. Firms in the process of downsizing are hiring outplacement experts to ease departing staffers into new jobs. Other counseling services provide guidance for those who want to change careers on their own initiative. Dr. Helen Harkness, who operates Career Design Associates in Garland, a suburb of Dallas, is on the leading edge. Her typical client is an individual who has some degree of job burn-out, coupled with a mid-life crisis or unresolved personal issues. They are searching for meaning, money, creativity, and control through a major career change. Dr. Harkness, who started in the teaching profession, has gone through career transformation herself. She uses a series of workshops to help people learn about themselves and where they might find a happy fit. The most important task, however, is psychological: overcoming fear of an uncertain future and learning to accept a new identity. Helen Harkness says that people must pass through stages. Only when the pain of your present situation becomes truly excessive can you overcome the fear of breaking with the past. After that, it's a matter of building confidence and self-esteem to take on new challenges. There's also a lot of practical advice along the way. Scared of making mistakes in a new professional setting? Silly you; all successful people commit errors along the way. Are you perhaps afraid that you're too old for a major change? Wrong again. Considering current life span trends, you should mentally deduct about 15 years of your age when looking at jobs. That's because functional and chronological age are not necessarily congruent. Dr. Harkness, who looks mature but won't mention her own age, says that old dogs do learn new tricks. We'll return to this topic when we take up the 21st century life cycle in the concluding chapter.

Telecommuting, mentioned earlier, may be particularly well suited for mature workers who are disabled or have transportation problems. New, user-friendly communication technologies are making it possible for them to work at home. The government's Bureau of Labor Statistics found that working at home is nearly twice as prevalent among people aged 45 to 54 as among those between the ages of 25 to 34. Other positive factors may be greater maturity and self-motivation, not to mention the fact that older folks are less likely to face distractions from youngsters at home. Since results, not appearance, are the ideal employment criteria, discrimination based on age or disability is sharply diminished. Meanwhile, employers are able to save on office space, furnishings, utilities, and the like.

If money is not a problem, the later years may offer unique opportunities for self-development. For example, prudent individuals, reaping the benefits of fiscal and health investments described in Chapter 4, have a far greater chance to do the things they had only dreamed about during their working lives. In a survey of its membership, the AARP noted "...powerful forces [are] operating in a kind of late-developing restlessness. People talk of seizing a chance to realize a lifelong dream or fulfill some inner goal." The study named a number of examples: a teacher who became a commercial pilot, a secretary who turned into a private investigator, and a banker who became a casino blackjack dealer. These may be the adventurous few, but it illustrates the positive potential for aging in the next century.

Finally, there are satisfying alternatives to paying jobs for those who have achieved financial independence. Retirement experts advise working age adults to develop satisfying hobbies at an early age. Constructive activities, in a retirement setting, help to compensate for the loss of prestige and satisfaction of a job well done. Volunteering is perhaps the single best way to maintain a sense of self-worth and satisfying social contacts. The opportunities are boundless. SCORE, for instance, stands for Senior Corps of Retired Executives who use their many years of business experience to counsel folks who are just getting started in business. There are also programs for foster grandparents, environmental monitors, health care assistants, and the like. Don't forget that the new generation of elderly will be much better educated and healthier than most senior citizens who came before them. There is no reason why they should not give a hand to Generation X. Some, like SCORE, are government programs; others are administered through churches, civic organizations, and the like. Considering the many problems our nation will face in the next century, it makes sense to get help and advice from the legions of retirees. Both generations will be well served.

Chapter 3

Where's My Check? Forecasting Pension and Social Security Benefits

Do yourself a favor: Call 1-800-772-1213. It's a toll-free number for the Social Security Administration where you can request a Personal Earnings and Benefit Statement. Social Security then directs its computer in Baltimore to audit your record and provide a projection of retirement and disability benefits. With a current salary of around $50,000, I could expect to collect somewhere around $1200 a month at age 65. Your benefits will depend on your own earning record over a lifetime, your marital status, and some other factors. On the average, most people currently don't draw much more than $800, and those who have lifetime low earnings will have to make do with benefits around $500 a month. The check is a little bigger if you're married. Maximum benefits in 1996 topped out at $1248.

Once you've done that, contact the personnel office where you work and check out the status of your pension account. Most folks are surprised at how small their monthly pension checks will be. By doing this now, you can avoid a nasty surprise a few years down the road.

Now, add up what it costs to live in your town. I'm certain that rent, food, clothing, transportation, utilities, medical expenses, and all the rest far exceed the amount you'll have coming in. Unless you have a very substantial pension or other sources of income, your Social Security check will hardly provide a decent lifestyle in your "Golden Years." So many Americans talk longingly of early retirement. Beware! That wish is likely to come true but not in the way we wanted. We already know that technological and demographic trends are on a collision course. The demand for workers will decline just as Baby Boomers hit the top earning plateau in their careers. Firings of upper and middle managers are often disguised as "early retirement." With a long life left to live, what do you do now?

False Sense of Security?

Retirement experts talk about the "three-legged stool" when discussing sources of income in later life. In order to maintain pre-retirement life style, people should have Social Security plus some form of pension and personal savings. Some ultra-thrifty folks may even have a fourth leg in the form of a military pension or supplementary savings account. The situation becomes precarious when the stool has only two or, heaven forbid, one leg. The problem for most of us is over-reliance on pensions and Social Security, neither of which we directly control. Many people have no idea what their benefits will be and don't even want to know! "I'll worry about that when I get there" is the prevailing attitude. Little do they know that, even when combined, pensions and Social Security result in very austere retirement income. Moreover, both are headed toward cutback in the future. This chapter summarizes evolving trends, focusing on future shortfalls which in most cases can only be remedied with substantially higher savings and investments on our part. But that comes in Chapter 4.

Pension Plans in Transition

Since virtually everyone is covered by Social Security, folks paying into company pension plans count themselves among the privileged few. This is a dangerous delusion. Except for high-level executives and their "golden parachutes," most working people can expect only a modest payout from their pension funds. While the statistics are not exact, a recent survey of pension plans yielded only a 25 percent return rate of pre-retirement income. Pensions in many ways reflect the economic and demographic trends summarized in Chapter 1. Here's what's happening.

During the go-go years of economic expansion after World War II, there was a general labor shortage. This resulted in high wages and generous fringe benefits. Many employers, and sometimes even labor unions, offered workers a Defined Benefits Plan pension. After a minimum period of service, say 10 years, employees were guaranteed monthly checks at a specified retirement age. The dollar amount was calculated with a formula which combined salary levels with total years of service. At the time, businesses could not imagine that growth rates would ever slow down, or that the arrival of the information age would dramatically reduce their work force. It was assumed that hordes of newly hired workers would steadily replenish the coffers of company retirement funds. As it turned out, businesses were forced to reassess their pension liabilities in the 70s and 80s. For one thing, the ratio of prospective pensioners to current workers would be much higher than anticipated. Worse yet, longer life spans would increase pension and medical benefit burdens. Some declining industries, like passenger railroads, could even see the day when pensioners outnumbered current employees! While panic is too strong a term, corporations focused their "downsizing" policies on middle and upper-income workers to avoid future pension liabilities. The government, incidentally, followed essentially the same policy in trimming the armed forces after the Cold War.

What workers did not know was that both company and union pension accounts were frequently used as slush funds. The provider had a moral obligation to invest these funds wisely, so they would grow and increase future benefits. Jimmy Hoffa of the Teamsters Union, and others like him, severely abused the members' pension funds. Corporations were not totally innocent either. There were too many risky, questionable investments. In some cases pension funds were used to fund mergers and acquisitions which, while boosting the bottom line, ironically also resulted in the firing of many workers who were unwittingly financing the deal. The worst case scenario was company bankruptcy. All too often, long-time workers saw their benefits evaporate into thin air.

In 1974, Congress yielded to union pressure and reformed the system. Without going into detail, this included rules making companies more accountable, while creating a federal Pension Benefit Guarantee Corporation. This PBGC has similarities to the FDIC, which insures savings accounts. Companies with pension plans would contribute to the fund, and if bankruptcy occurred, such as with Pan Am Airways, PBGC would protect employees' pension rights. Ultimate obligations were shifted to the government.

Do it Yourself Pensions Arrive

The 1974 reforms addressed not only employers but also moved in the direction of offering workers more personal participation in terms of risk and opportunity. The resulting Individual Retirement Account (IRA) largely put the monkey back on the employee's back. There are several variations, all of which offer an inviting tax break: Current contributions are tax deferred, while future pay-outs are taxed at presumably lower retiree brackets. There are three variations. First, the so-called "Keough Plan" applies to self-employed persons only, allowing them, hopefully with the aid of an accountant or financial advisor, to set up a personal pension plan based on investments of the individual's choice. The second, a plain IRA, is for people who are employed, even perhaps covered by a pension plan, and allows them to make contributions toward a personal retirement nest egg. The third, called the 401(k), after provision in the tax code, is like the others except that it is administered by an employer. Many companies kick in a supplement to the workers' 401(k) plan as a fringe benefit. It can also be used as a vehicle for profit sharing.

IRAs offer several other advantages. First, they are more "portable," so when a worker changes jobs his accumulated savings follow; secondly, there is no legal way for an employer to borrow from an individual's account; and finally, IRAs provide the nation with much-needed investment funds when contributions flow into the stock and bond markets.

Slowly, but surely, the defined benefit plans of yesteryear are being replaced by these 401(k), or Defined Contribution Plans. In essence, even though employers still make investment decisions for their participants, they are not liable for any specified pay-outs. That depends on how well the fund has been managed and how much gets accumulated over the years. On the one hand, people are no longer subject to a predetermined company system; on the other hand, it calls for some painful personal decisions in terms of how much to save for an uncertain future. We will return to this topic in the next chapter, which covers investments.

Are you a government employee? Then consider yourself lucky! Compared to their counterparts in private industry, government workers may receive lower salaries, but they are compensated with more security, including solid pension plans. If we include the armed forces, state, local, and federal employees, these people account for a hefty 15 percent of the total U.S. work force. Many workers cite pension benefits among their primary reasons for having chosen public service. Why are government pensions so high? It seems that elected officials have a natural aversion to giving civil service employees raises. That requires taxes. To make it up, they can sweeten workers' pension benefits which, in effect, passes the tax obligation to future generations of citizens and politicians. New York City's bankruptcy in 1975 featured many villains, and outrageously generous benefits for retired municipal workers were to blame for a big chunk of the accumulated deficit. This is also a problem at the federal level.

Until recent reforms, military personnel could count on half of their base salary plus health care and other fringe benefits after only 20 years of service. These pending retirement obligations for our large Cold War active and reserve military forces figure prominently in the crushing federal debt described in the first chapter. The sum of congressional pensions, frequently heard about in the news, is chump change in terms of total federal obligations. Finally, most government pensions feature COLA, a Cost of Living Adjustment. This means that pensions are constantly ratcheted upward in response to inflation as measured by the consumer price index. Unlike business policies which change according to the prevailing economic winds, these government commitments are mandated by law and nearly impossible to cancel.

The Uncertain Future of Pensions

The future offers little comfort to individuals. Sensing austere demographic and economic trends, management will continue to seek relief from future pension obligations. This is seen in the increasing reliance on part-time and temporary help, "outsourcing" labor operations, and offering mid-level employees "early out" lump sum severance agreements in lieu of pensions. Labor statistics tell that the number of workers covered by company pension plans has been dropping steadily since the 70s. Many of those companies which retained pension plans are moving from the defined benefit to the defined contribution schemes, effectively shifting the risk to the workers.

Another disturbing trend is the transfer of pension contributions from employers to insurance companies. If the system works, insurance companies manage and invest the funds and eventually provide pensioners with annuities. Employers are relieved of the obligation; meanwhile, pensioners must be concerned about reckless management by the insurance company. When massive Executive Life Insurance Company collapsed in 1991, retirees took a deep breath when learning that an insurance company, unlike their business, was not covered by the Pension Benefit Guarantee Corporation!

The last piece of bad news is that companies have been using pension contributions for a wide range of purposes, handing the retirement kitty an IOU. Workers are seldom aware of this "underfunding" practice until there is a financial crisis and accounting takes place. Bankruptcy is the worst case scenario. When Pan American Airlines "crashed" in 1991, its single biggest debt was to the employees' pension fund. Considering that the pension obligation then passed to the government's Pension Guarantee system, the workers were safe, but Pan Am's debt was in effect shifted to the American taxpayers. Other corporations are deliberately splitting profitable and unprofitable operations with only one expected to survive. Can you guess which one gets the pension obligations? It is said that a whole number of bankruptcies and "reorganizations," to use the business lingo, have been engineered with this dark purpose in mind.

Ultimately, taxpayers and pensioners must keep their eyes on the soundness of the PBGC. Periodically the agency publishes a status report. At the end of 1995, the PBGC reported that the 50 largest underfunded companies were $64 billion short, double the amount from 1994. The list reads like an honor roll of American industry. Other factors such as interest rates and the general health of the economy also play a role. The fund is usually in the red, and unless company underfunding and the number of business failures are reversed, it may find itself in the same unenviable position recently occupied by the Federal Savings and Loan Insurance Corporation. If you recall, the taxpayers bailed out the mismanaged S & L industry. Will the nation be so generous if this retirement fund goes belly-up? Be prepared to witness a battle royal between angry taxpayers and frustrated retirees.

Social Security: Rock or Quicksand?

In the history of our nation, few social programs have been as popular and successful as Social security. Nowadays, opinion researchers say that more young people believe in flying saucers than in Social Security in their future. A crisis of confidence is at hand. The problem for most of us is understanding the system. It is enormously complex, and even the experts widely disagree on what Social Security is all about. For instance, is Social Security a welfare or a pension plan? The answer is: both. It was originally conceived as a publicly-funded, anti-poverty safety net for people unable to work and later transformed into a pension plan under vastly different demographic and economic circumstances. Now the tide is changing again. The Program is beginning to shed its pension function and will ultimately return to its welfare role in the next century. Despite the confusion, the big picture of Social Security's growth, current crises, and future can be well understood in terms of the demographic, economic, and related trends described in the opening chapter.

Why Social Security?

The birth of Social Security in 1935 was part of the government's "New Deal" policies to combat the ravages of the Depression. In fact, today's program was a relatively small part of a large legislative package designed to provide unemployed, disabled, and elderly workers with a bare bones living allowance. The retirement provisions applied to all workers over 65, which in the thirties was the approximate normal life span. There were also benefit provisions for disabled workers, widows, and dependent children of participants. At that time, there were roughly 15 workers contributing to the Social Security trust fund for each retiree eligible to draw benefits.

The story of Miss Ida Fuller, who became the first recipient, is quite instructive for the future. After having contributed less than $100.00 over the minimum five-year period, this legal secretary retired in 1940 with initial benefits of $22.00 per month. When Miss Fuller died in 1975, past the age of 100, she had collected total benefits of more than $20,000 from Social Security!

Unlike in some other countries, our system operates on a "pay-as-you-go" basis. The benefits for each generation of retirees are paid from the Social Security taxes of current workers, who, in turn, would be supported by their successors. This worked great for Miss Fuller and her successors during the great economic boom and employment expansion. With so many people paying so much money into the system, the government was able to expand the benefits far beyond its original humble intent. Imperceptibly, Social Security was transformed within the span of a generation from a worker-supported welfare fund into a universal pension plan. Medicare, a similarly financed health care program for retirees, was added in 1965. Even with inflation factored in, that epoch's rapid employment growth and prosperity made it possible for people to get far more out of the system than they had ever paid in, according to government statistics. The average married 65-year-old man, who retired in the early 80s, could expect to receive benefits five times greater than his contributions. No wonder Social Security was so popular!

Demographics, Automation, and the Crisis of the 1980s

Two major developments upset the apple cart in the early 80s. One was the realization that the relatively small "Baby Bust" generation would be incapable of generously supporting the large numbers of long-living Boomers who would retire ahead of them. This is graphically presented by figure 1. The second major development was the emerging post-industrial economy, hinting that automation would further break down this taxpaying work force. Sensing a future meltdown of the system, the Reagan administration in 1983 called on the noted economist Alan Greenspan to study the problem. The Greenspan Commission offered several Band-aids. First, Social Security taxes would be substantially raised to accumulate a surplus in the 21st century for aging Boomers. Secondly, the retirement eligibility age would be gradually raised to keep in step with longer life spans. Thirdly, early retirement would also be discouraged. Finally, future benefits would be reduced, particularly for those with post-retirement jobs or high incomes from other sources. A combination of these economic measures were created in the hope of safeguarding the system well into the future.

Another threat to the system emerged in 1990. By law, all Social Security funds must be invested in U.S. Government securities, typically bonds issued to cover the federal deficit. Because the money then gets mingled with the general fund, it reduces the deficit until the bonds come due. Senator Daniel Patrick Moynihan, of New York, shocked the public by proclaiming that the huge Baby Boomer surpluses, set aside for the next century, were being used to mask a much deeper federal deficit than the official numbers indicated. The quandary of debt was discussed in an earlier chapter. The serious problem will come in the 2010s and 2020s when the bonds come due to

Figure 1

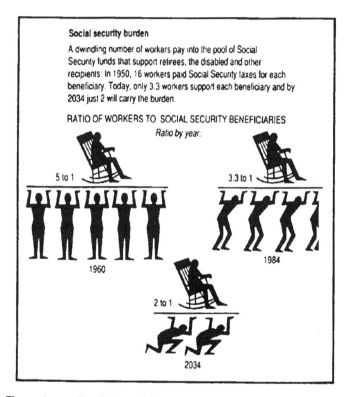

Figure 1   The Burden of Social Security (*Source:* Board of Social Security Trust Funds)

finance retirement benefits. At that point, Social Security will begin to run large annual deficits. Figure 2 presents government estimates for the next half century.

Since the government is currently using Social Security surplus funds to pay for other things, it must either raise more general taxes or drastically cut spending if it intends to make good on its obligations to Baby Boomer retirees. Since both alternatives are politically unacceptable to the general public, prospective retirees have ample cause to fear that some form of default, inflation, or other economic calamity will suck the system dry between 2030 and 2040. Generation X, the Baby Busters, have an even greater cause for alarm. They will not only have the burden of dealing with the debt their elders created, they will also likely face a bankrupt Social Security kitty in their later years. Moynihan and his supporters urged Congress to bite the bullet and take Social Security funds out of the general budget, or at least reduce Social Security taxes, since they were being unfairly used to replace other revenues. As you can imagine, Moynihan's effort to prevent our Social Security nest egg from turning into a bad loan was defeated by our collective shortsighted concern with the problems of the moment.

Some Myths and Realities

No wonder we're so worried and confused. Popular misconceptions, coupled with opportunistic politicians taking advantage of our fears and insecurities instead of facing the real problems, greatly threaten the system. It seems that even fiscally conservative "tax cutters" make generous elder entitlements part of their election campaigns. Instead of looking for someone to blame, we should focus at the root causes. Unfortunately, the real imperatives of future demographic and economic change are seldom articulated.

One misconception is that Social Security is sort of a savings account to which people make deposits and eventually withdraw what they deposited. A number of other countries

Social Security Annual Operating Budget

(Billions of Dollars)

Social Security now has a small annual cash surplus but will begin to run large annual cash deficits around 2015

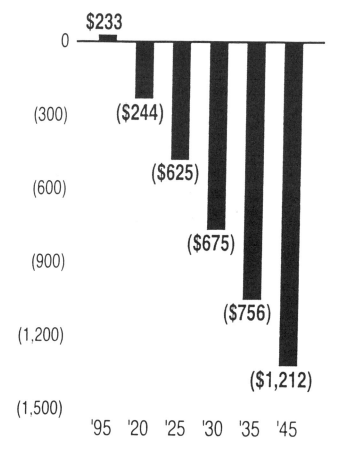

$233

0

(300)   ($244)

($625)

(600)

($675)

(900)

($756)

(1,200)

($1,212)

(1,500)

'95 '20 '25 '30 '35 '45

Source: Social Security Administration, 1995; *Will America Grow Up Before It Grows Old?*

have such "fully-funded" systems; each retiree draws exclusively on what he or she had deposited over a lifetime. By contrast, America's retirees depend on the contributions of others, which in the past usually meant higher pay-outs than taxes paid. Still, people believe that they have earned their benefits and tenaciously oppose realistic adjustments. Figure 3 illustrates the excess of benefits over contributions for a typical couple retiring in the mid-90s. After the 1983 Social Security reforms, the pay-out ratio will gradually decline, so that average benefits for retirees of the next century will roughly match their contributions or only slightly exceed them.

There is also a profound misunderstanding about the actual amounts of Social Security checks. As we learned at the beginning of this chapter, those folks who think the amount will provide adequate retirement income are in for a shock. On the average, it would replace only slightly more than half the income from the last pay check. Here's where it gets complicated. Even though high and low earners paid premiums at the same rate, a "Robin Hood factor" provides poorer retirees a much higher proportion of benefits than their wealthier counterparts. Bigger contributors still get bigger checks, but the disparity is reduced by padding the checks of the little people. Among other things, Social Security turns out to be a subtle anti-poverty program for the elderly! Another adjustment comes in the form of COLA, the annual Cost-of-Living-Adjustment keyed to the Consumer Price Index. In times of inflation, the index rises and results in bigger checks. Low inflation in the mid-90s encouraged Washington to temporarily freeze the COLA, or at least refigure the Consumer Price Index downward to slow the growth of future obligations. Defenders of the current system called this "cutting Social Security." Judge for yourself. Figure 4 shows how the cumulative effect of these adjustments, like compound interest, creates a huge difference in the long run.

Figure 3

Payback in Excess of Contributions*

A typical couple retiring today will receive far more in Social
Security and Medicare benefits than the value of their prior
contributions plus interest

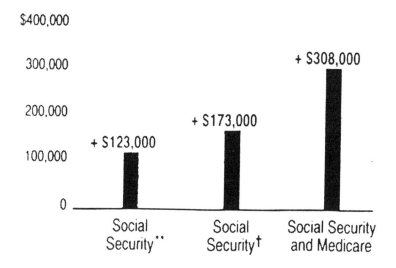

$400,000

300,000   + $308,000

200,000   + $173,000

100,000   + $123,000

0

Social   Social   Social Security
Security**   Security†   and Medicare

* Contributions plus interest in constant 1993 dollars
** Benefits received in excess of prior employer and employee contributions
† Benefits received in excess of employee contributions alone

Source: *Retooling Social Security for the 21st Century*

How Come My Check Is So Small?

Are you shortchanging yourself in terms of future benefits? Max (not his real name) does periodic carpentry and paint-
ing work at my home. When the job is finished, he usually asks
for cash rather than a check made out to his business. Why? He
and many others who work as domestics, in restaurants and
other service trades are typically self-employed and operate in
the "cash economy," where money is untraceable and untaxable.
Dodging Social Security taxes may put a few more dollars in
Max's pocket at the moment; however, I doubt that he has an
alternative savings plan for the future. When his first benefit
check arrives, he'll probably be scratching his head, wondering
why others get so much more. My friend Betty, who works as
a self-employed artist, has figured it out and is deliberately fat-
tening her account to avoid such an unpleasant future surprise.

A large number of immigrants are also likely to fall
between the cracks. Chapter 1 described how waves of immigrants are changing the face of America. So what does this have
to do with retirement and Social Security? It seems that many
immigrants come from traditional cultures where large intergenerational families take care of elders. My town has a large
community of Southeast Asians,who came as refugees after the
Vietnam War. Traditional Asian culture involves veneration of
the elderly, and some of my Vietnamese and Laotian friends are
shocked by the lack of respect older Americans get. The concept of independent and self-supporting senior citizens is quite
unique to modern industrial societies. It should also be pointed
out that many new arrivals tend to work in family businesses or
sweat shops run by other immigrants who dispense with such
formalities as payroll deduction, benefit plans, and the like.
Serious problems will arise in the next generation when young
people become "Americanized" in terms of higher mobility,
career aspirations, and release from the tyranny of traditional

Figure 4

For Social Security, Potential Erosion˙

The average monthly Social Security benefit paid to those retired by December 31, 1984*

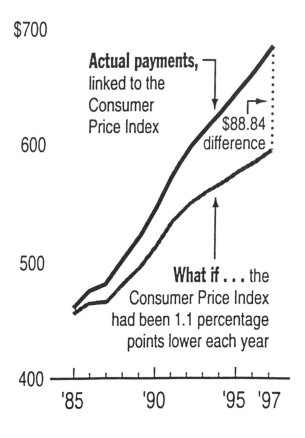

$700

Actual payments, ⌐ linked to the Consumer Price Index

$88.84 difference

600

500

What if . . . the Consumer Price Index had been 1.1 percentage points lower each year

400

'85 '90 '95 '97

* Average benefits vary by retirement date.

Source: Social Security Administration, 1996

family authority. Consequently, aging immigrants face a double whammy in the next century: Their extended family support is evaporating and they have not accumulated the personal financial resources of the American peer generation. The same dilemma, by the way, is faced by aging nuns, monks, and others who have given their lives to religious vocations which have become marginalized by the church mainstream.

That brings us to Supplementary Security Income (SSI), meant to help those who are ineligible for Social Security or whose benefits were too minute for survival. Originally implemented by the Nixon administration in 1974, SSI was a pure welfare program granting any needy individual an income at the survival level. This federal program is available to young and old alike and grants benefits to cover the gap between a person's income and the official poverty level. Food stamps and other welfare benefits are also tied in. As you can imagine, there are currently many elderly people whose Social Security benefits are so low, they must apply for SSI to make ends meet. Unfortunately, this program carries the stigma of "welfare," which Americans greatly detest. Nevertheless, SSI is close to the original concept of Social Security and may become an important source of support for many elderly people if pension provisions of the current system are down-scaled or privatized.

Is Privatization the Answer?

If you don't trust Uncle Sam, you might be interested to know that there are proposals to privatize the whole system by converting the current trust fund structure into "Personal Savings Accounts." Members of the business, banking, and securities industries are backing Conservative "think tanks," like the CATO Institute and the Concord Coalition, which recommend funneling future Social Security taxes into the private securities market. Organized along the lines of a super IRA, the proposal would side-step those suspect U.S. bonds in favor of high-earning stocks, corporate bonds, and real estate invesments.

They claim that this form of "capital formation" would spark an investment fire, boosting American business productivity, while generating enormous profits for retirees.

Critics of privatization contend that such profitability is far from sure in today's global economy, because investors' fortunes are at the mercy of market swings. Look at Chile, where the dictator Pinochet established such a system in 1981. The good news is that Chile's booming free market economy has provided handsome returns on these investments. The bad news is that the private enterprises, which administer the program, are gouging the public, earning a rate of 22 percent per year while charging an exorbitant 13 percent service fee. While economists like to talk in terms of long-term averages, you should remember that the business cycle involves periodic up and down swings. Figure 5 illustrates how rates of return for the Chilean investment companies have fluctuated since the inception of the program. While everyone cheers for a rising market, few people can stomach the yo-yo effect when their futures are on the line.

Obviously, the U.S. asset management and investment industry salivates at the earnings prospects and is aggressively promoting it in policy circles. Aside from high commissions, what are potential problems? First, if everyone starts paying into an Individual Savings Account, how will we pay for those who are currently in the system and have a legal claim on the contributions of the generation behind them? Secondly, a privatized system would dangerously widen the gap between rich and poor elderly in the absence of equalizing formulas which currently exist. Finally, it is unclear whether the nation's securities markets could digest the flood tide of funds which would come in. Rather than "privatizing" Social Security, we might end up "nationalizing" Wall Street.

Coming Full Circle in the Next Century

Having studied prevailing demographic and economic trends, we now realize that Social Security must inevitably

Figure 5

Fluctuations in Chilean Retirement Investment Funds

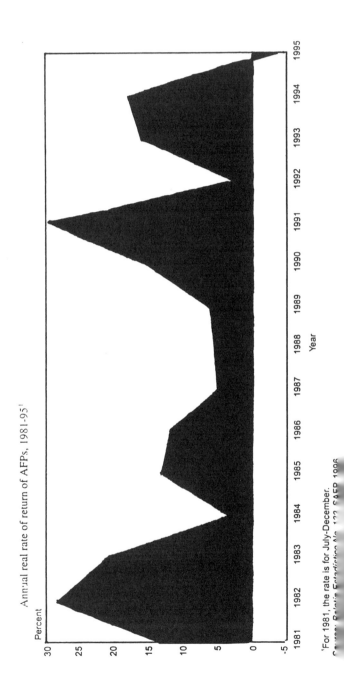

Annual real rate of return of AFPs, 1981-95[1]

[1] For 1981, the rate is for July-December.

Source: Boletín Estadístico No. 132, SAFP, 1996.

trends, we now realize that Social Security must inevitably return to its roots as a safety net for economically-distressed citizens. The demographic and economic booms in the middle of the 20th century were somewhat of an historical "detour," as were the expansive social policies spawned by that era. Future historians will shake their heads over a society which felt so rich that it used public funds to subsidize the retirement of millionaires. But then again, who would want to break such a habit?

The Baby Bust, an economic slowdown, and the arrival of the information age in the latter part of the century woke us up to the fact that the standards and expectations of previous decades no longer apply. A rising public debt also served as a sobering warning against excessive future generosity. Figure 6 shows how entitlements and interest payments are eating into our economy. The 1983 reforms of Social Security were a step in the right direction, but only one step. Considering the unfolding trends, the government must accelerate the Greenspan Commission recommendations if the system is to survive. In practical terms, future austerity will mean that the system will return to its originally intended function as a safety net or anti-poverty insurance. Naturally, this will be hard for some folks to swallow, especially those who had counted on an ever-growing Social Security largesse. As expectations are scaled back, the taxes will be also. Generation X, which seems to have so little to gain, will see to that. On the other hand, the nation's tradition of care and respect for the elderly will not allow us to abandon those with genuine and pressing needs. There is even a good possibility that Social Security of the future will be merged with the Supplemental Security Income system.

Projected Federal Spending as a percentage of GDP

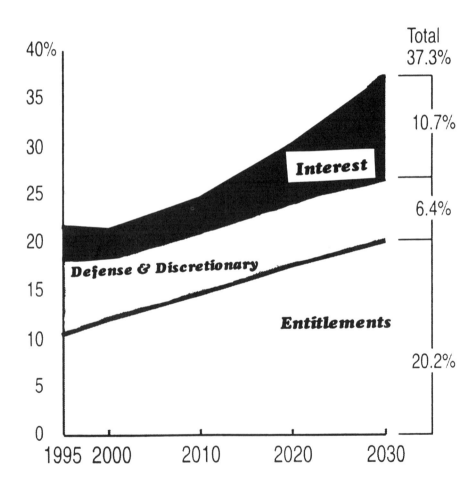

Source: Bipartisan Commission on Entitlements, 1995

Chapter 4

INVESTING: Take Charge of Your Own Future.

Thirty thousand dollars for dinner and a movie? Byron, my tax accountant, claims that you can accumulate that much for investment purposes with a simple change in your recreation habits. According to his calculations, an average couple might treat themselves twice a month to pizza at a restaurant, followed by a movie. Assuming that the average cost for the evening comes to $25, that same couple could have stayed home and spent $9 for an oven-cooked pizza and a video rental. If the monthly savings of $32 were invested at a measly six percent annual interest rate, these folks would have accumulated $30,000 after 30 years! Silly as it sounds, Byron's example illustrates the importance of thrift and the power of compound interest when it comes to investing.

The preceding chapters offer two important lessons. First, both Social Security and pension benefit plans face greater austerity in the economic and demographic environment of the 21st century. Secondly, both government and business sector employment policies are headed in opposite directions. While government extends retirement eligibility to protect Social Security, business often finds it expedient to release workers long before retirement age. So, who gets caught in the middle? You do.

Now you know why it's so important to take charge of your own future by investing. We will now consider **Investment** in a larger sense. Sure it involves setting aside savings for the future, but it also includes a number of other things. Knowledge, undoubtedly, is at the top of the list. Time and effort spent on learning about the future are rewarded with priceless insights into your prospective needs and resources. This, in turn, should be a prime factor in making current decisions affecting your job, savings, home purchases, etc. Good health is another investment overlooked by many. Without your health, all other aspects of life quickly become unmanageable, not to mention expensive. Unfortunately, many folks still think they can abuse their bodies and then get a fast overhaul. Medical care will be rationed in the next century, and individuals will have to take greater responsibility for maintaining a healthy lifestyle. So why not start now?

Marriage, believe it or not, is another great investment in the future. Government statistics indicate that married people are wealthier and live longer than their single counterparts. There are a number of reasons for this. First, all of us know the old wisdom that by sharing the same household, two can live as cheaply as one. Secondly, various government policies give favorable treatment to families. Finally, there is the benefit of pooling two incomes. Since real wages have been falling for

Figure 1

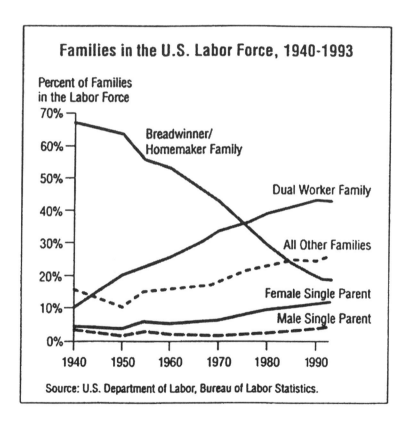

Families in the U.S. Labor Force, 1940-1993

Percent of Families
in the Labor Force

- Breadwinner/Homemaker Family
- Dual Worker Family
- All Other Families
- Female Single Parent
- Male Single Parent

70%
60%
50%
40%
30%
20%
10%
0%

1940 1950 1960 1970 1980 1990

Source: U.S. Department of Labor, Bureau of Labor Statistics.

many workers since the 1970s, the dual income household has saved the middle-American lifestyle. Figure 1 shows that the "breadwinner-homemaker" family has almost disappeared over the last half century. It has been replaced by the "dual earner" family. Those same government statistics, by the way, also point out that many people are opting out of marriage. Whether by divorce, or choice not to marry, the number of single households is growing rapidly. Children in these households are most vulnerable to poverty, while even middle-class single, adults typically face a far less secure future than their married friends.

Family Inheritance: A Dubious Nest Egg

What usually distinguishes prosperous people from their less affluent neighbors? Hard work? Not necessarily. The fortunate ones typically got a leg up the old-fashioned way, with some form of inheritance. Although folks don't like to talk about it, most look forward to a small windfall in their middle years. Unfortunately, if their parents belonged to the Baby Boomer generation, the future prospects are not so bright. Why?

The Baby Boom generation worked hard and played hard; meanwhile, it also spent hard. The previous generation learned the value of thrift at the hands of the Great Depression. This prewar generation was both flinty and self-reliant. Baby Boomers, on the other hand, grew up in a time of spectacular economic growth, which was reflected in their profligate lifestyle and casual attitude toward money. There was always tomorrow, or so it seemed. As a result, this generation is simultaneously responsible for high personal debt and relatively low personal savings. Lack of savings spells bad news for folks in their later years. It also deprives the general economy of investment capital, not to mention Generation X, which can expect very little in the way of inheritance to finance its start in life. Can we blame government for this savings gap? First, government fiscal policies of the period followed roughly the same spendthrift pattern. Then, Social Security benefits and pensions, which seemed to grow ever larger, lulled people into complacence about the need for personal savings. Tax policies, too, rewarded spending rather than saving. The "Supply Side" economic doctrine of the 1980s relied on spending to generate continued economic growth; savings were assumed to follow automatically. Economists now agree that there were far too many reasons not to save during those heady economic times. The 21st century will witness government policies which encourage thrift. But it might be too late for many folks.

The prospect of inheritance, whether it is a house, stock portfolio or cash, is what sets middle and upper income people apart from those in lesser circumstances. It often grants a level of security which earnings alone could not provide. However, you should be aware that the inheritance prospects differ from generation to generation. The process can be best understood by applying the "life cycle theory" of the economist Franco Modigliani. Traditionally, people accumulate wealth by saving during their working lives, and then spend down this wealth to finance their cost of living after retirement. The next generation covered any shortfall as support, or received the excess as inheritance.

Baby Boomers who received inheritances in the 1980s and 1990s got a lucky break and did much better than any previous generation. Let's explain why. First, their prewar parents generation, which had experienced the Depression, saved with a vengeance. But as they became elderly, generous pensions, Social Security, and Medicare benefits short-circuited the spend-down process, allowing a greater accumulation of wealth for their heirs. Furthermore, assets of this generation, specifically real estate values, had grown enormously during the Boomers' nesting years. On top of that, real estate assets of elderly people, whether rich or poor, have always enjoyed tax abatement. In a way, then, young people, through rising Social

Security taxes, helped protect assets that the lucky few would inherit.

Let's not forget the effects of changing family dynamics, such as frequent divorce and remarriage, on the inheritance process. When we exchanged life stories, Lisa, one of my co-workers, told me that her parents split shortly after she was born. Lisa stayed with her mother, who subsequently remarried and had three more children with her new spouse. Lisa's father also remarried and now has four children from the second marriage. Since everyone lives in different states, Lisa is not sure of her rights when her natural father passes away. Most likely, she'll be short-changed.

Or consider President Clinton, whose parents were each married four times and produced children in several of those unions. Can you imagine the potential confusion among the heirs? If there is any money in the estate, it would take a tribe of lawyers to untangle the competing claims. Now look around and count the number of your acquaintances who are in the same fix.

If you're a young Boomer, or worse—a Baby Buster, your inheritance prospects are further diminished by several other factors. Members of the Baby Boom generation not only failed to save sufficiently, they can also expect to live longer, spending down what little they have tucked away. The concept of "Reverse Mortgage," whereby elders can raise cash by selling the single largest asset, their home, will be discussed in Chapter 7. Furthermore, emerging government policies are designed to tap, rather than preserve, private estate wealth. For instance, until recently, even wealthy retirees could count on almost "free" hospitalization and doctors' visits courtesy of Medicare. The details of Medicare will be discussed in the next chapter. Suffice it to say, the near term insolvency of the system will force the administrators to look aggressively for funds to keep the system afloat. What better source than the accumulated assets of the recipients?

For a while, clever lawyers helped greedy prospective heirs to receive major assets from a seriously-ill, elderly relative. This, in effect, made the elderly person a pauper, eligible for public support, while their substantial estate had been quietly shuffled into the pockets of various heirs. Current laws no longer permit this practice and require a near total spend-down of assets before such public assistance can be granted. In the future this will also include "viatical settlements" of life insurance policies, where benefits are paid prior to death.

The state of Oregon has started an "asset recovery plan," whereby government nursing home costs can be deducted from a recipient's estate after death. Senior citizen lobbies have fought it, but other states are heading in the same direction. Considering how long medical technology can keep disabled people alive, there is no question that many future inheritances will be eaten up in this fashion. Then, when large numbers of Baby Boomers start hitting hospitals and nursing homes in the 2020s, depleted public assets may well force health care authorities to bill their offspring! Ultimately, the large inheritances, accumulated during the boom years of the 20th century, will have disappeared, to be replaced, perhaps, by a debt for the heirs to repay. Family members can expect a bill whenever a deceased relative receives some form of public assistance.

Show Me the Money! Learning to Invest

Obviously, neither pensions, nor Social Security, nor inheritance is a sure bet in the next century. That leaves only one option: taking the bull by the horns and initiating a personal investment program. The first task is to be informed. You can do this on your own by getting an investment guide written for the layman. Your local bookstore is likely to have a good stock of guides and manuals written by some of the most competent and respected financial experts in the country. A few are listed at the end of this book. Colleges and universities often offer non-credit courses on investment. It also makes sense to start paying attention to the business news in the media. Finally, you may contact a reputable broker, investment advisor, or other asset manager in your community.

Some things are to be avoided. Be wary of investments suggested by your advisor if he or she stands to profit by steering you into those investments. If possible, seek counsel from those who cannot profit from your investments. Their knowledge is valuable and justifies the fee. Getting life insurance is a good idea; however, experts advise against using insurance companies as investment vehicles. It adds more commissions and another layer of management between you and your nest egg.

Finally, avoid the temptations of "get rich quick" schemes which are so aggressively promoted by late-night television, telephone salesmen, etc. There are neither investment "secrets" nor "miracles." If you've done your homework and know about average rates of return, reputations of potential enterprises in which to invest, and other pertinent information, you'll be able to smell out the phonies. Remember, if it sounds too good to be true, it usually is. Here's the bottom line: Except for some mavericks, competent investment experts use a fairly standard base of information when calculating risk and opportunity. Things like inflation get factored in. They also tend to diversify and use a variety of hedges on the side of conservatism. This means that you shouldn't have to lose any sleep over these decisions.

Setting Goals and Making Choices

Investment advisors or guidebooks will give you a number of important things to keep in mind. Here's a nutshell summary. To begin with, you should consider your current age and how long you expect to be in the work force. Then, look ahead, and try to determine how much income you will need at retirement and how long you can expect to live. Don't forget spouses, children, or other special needs in the future. Remember, too, that most folks will need between 70 percent and 80 percent of their pre-retirement income to maintain a comfortable lifestyle; however, Social Security and pensions usually add up to only 50 percent or less. The other 20 percent or more of future income must come from some type of savings or investments.

The AARP's *Retirement Planning Workbook*, and other such books, feature tables which tell how much a family or single individual would have to set aside in order to reach that goal. The experts will tell you that it's a mistake to put off these calculations until retirement is at hand. The process should start much earlier. One reason is the phenomenon of compound interest and rolled-over dividends, both of which give enormous advantage to young investors. Figure 2 shows that even small sums, set aside on a regular basis, will snowball in the long run. Another reason for starting early is the uncertainty of the future job market as described in chapter 2. You may need to use your savings long before age 65!

While it's a good idea to start young, my friend Bruce, a leading local investment advisor, likes to tell folks that it's better later than never. One of Bruce's octogenarian clients recently came in grumbling about having missed lucrative investment opportunities in his seventies! Who knows, he may need it when he joins the growing number of centenarians.

So, where do you invest? The answer is easy. There is a broad consensus among investment experts that Individual Retirement Plans (IRA), particularly the 401(k) variation, are the best way to go. You will recall that the 4Ol(k) plan involves a deduction from each paycheck; you'll never miss it. To be sure, voluntary saving requires far too much self-discipline for most folks. Secondly, since the money is not taxable until withdrawal, the tax bite on your paycheck is reduced as well. Finally, this form of savings is "portable" and can be transferred when you change jobs. Most 4Ol(k) plans, incidentally, rely upon investment decisions of the employer who manages them. But not to worry. Most "sponsor directed plans," as they are

Figure 2

IT'S NEVER TOO LATE TO START

Start young. A look at the performance of $2,000
retirement plan investments over time at 4%
shows the value of starting early.

IN 1995 DOLLARS

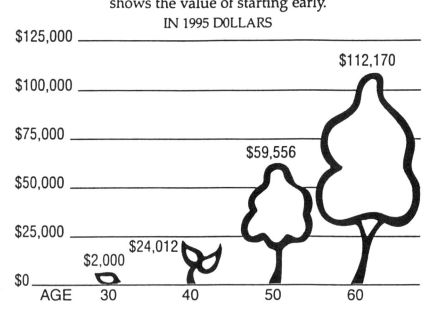

called, have fared better than those directed by individuals. The best ones, of course, are those where the employer adds profit sharing or matches employee contributions as a fringe benefit. If the 401(k) option is not available, turn to the personal IRA and Keough plans which require more self-discipline and investment decisions but are well worth the effort. The plans' tax advantage is a friendly reminder from the government that Social Security benefits are "headed south" for middle and upper-income folks in the next century.

Where should your IRA contributions go? Individuals are relatively free to decide, and may opt for anything from gold to real estate. Most experts, however, have chosen stocks and bonds, with a preference for the former, as the vehicle of choice. Individuals are advised to channel their contributions into well-diversified mutual funds. Company managed 401(k) plans do much the same, but often favor their own stock as a way of raising capital and encouraging employee loyalty. Many economists credit the stock market surge of the 1980s and 1990s to the steady influx of money from these retirement funds. It's been fun to watch, but what if the stock market crashes? First, there are not that many sound alternatives. Real estate, discussed in Chapter 7, is a very iffy investment during this transitional period. Fixed-income government securities, while basically sound, offer a smaller rate of return than what most people hope to get. Except for foolish investments, like gold, that leaves the commercial securities market as the single major investment vehicle.

Historically, stocks have outperformed all other investments. Figure 3 offers a comparative summary of the past 40-some years. Despite periodic ups and downs, there is a broad consensus that the stock and bond markets will continue to be solid investments. To begin with, the general economy is sound, and even those who have doubts about the future of American business can hedge by investing overseas. Secondly, individuals and fund managers tend to invest more conservatively and

Figure 3

Stocks win in a landslide

Over the last four decades, the return on equities has far outdistanced the return on bonds. Exception: the 1970s, when inflation soared and stocks suffered.

Cumulative total returns and inflation

	1950s	1960s	1970s	1980s	Whole period cumulative	annualized
Stocks (S&P 500)	486%	112%	77%	403%	10,968%	12.5%
Corporate bonds	11%	18%	83%	240%	713%	5.4%
Treasury bonds	-1%	16%	71%	227%	544%	4.8%
Treasury bills	20%	46%	84%	134%	661%	5.2%
Inflation	25%	28%	103%	65%	434%	4.3%

USN&WR – Basic Data: T Rowe Price Associates Inc.; Ibbotson Associates. Standard & Poor's

avoid speculation when dealing with retirement money. This means putting money into solid "blue chip" companies rather than volatile and chancy instruments like futures, margin purchases, and other derivatives which sometimes give the market a headache. The mechanics of IRA and mutual fund investment also discourage people from jumping in and out of the market, which had been a source of instability in the past. After all, if you withdraw funds from the market, what will you do with them? Consequently, the amount of money in stock and bond mutual funds rose from approximately $77 billion in 1982 to nearly $2 trillion in 1995, according to Wall Street figures. Meanwhile, there are now more mutual funds than companies listed on the New York Stock Exchange. So, as the Baby Boomers continue to pump their pension money into the stock market, everyone can ride the wave into the 21st century.

Problems could arise, however, around 2015 or 2020, when those same investors reach retirement age and start selling their stocks and bonds to raise cash for their retirement incomes. Logically, this should set off a selling panic, where everyone would try to sell while there are still buyers left.

The experts are divided on this question. However, the optimistic ones point to the fact that the "sell off" will be so gradual that it will not cause a stampede. Furthermore, maturing X-ers will be building their portfolios at that time. Even in the mid-90s, individual exposure to stocks in proportion to total financial assets was only 23 percent compared to a high of 36 percent in 1969. Saturation has clearly not taken place. Finally, don't count out the international dimension. If bargains become available, people from rapidly growing overseas economies will snap them up and stabilize our markets.

Are You Investing Enough?

Is it possible that your various retirement resources, including your company-sponsored IRA, are still insufficient for your future well-being? Yes, indeed. You will recall from earlier chapters that government needs to trim entitlement

Figure 4
How will inflation affect your future?

	1968	Today	Future year 2005	Inflation 4%
Gallon of gas	$0.33	$1.27	$1.74	
Loaf of bread	$0.43	$1.22	$1.67	
Movie ticket	$1.75	$7.26	$9.94	
Refrigerator	$400	$1,564	$2,140	

Your need		$100,000	$136,857

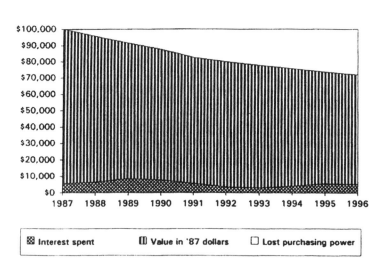

Source: American Express Financial Services

benefits in the next century. Don't forget about inflation; figure 4 illustrates how only modest inflation could erode the purchasing power of your nest egg. In addition, many retirement plans assume a maximum age of 85. If you really expect to be among the centenarians, stash away more money for those platinum years!

Everyone agrees on the need to salt away even more; but where, for heaven's sake, do you get the money? Most of us are glad to make it from payday to payday. Perhaps you can profit from the advice of Thomas Stanley and William Danko's best seller, *The Millionaire Next Door: The Surprising Secrets of America's Wealthy.* Building wealth, according to them, is simply a matter of living below your means and investing what you don't spend. The authors' research revealed that typical U.S. millionaires were self-employed and earned roughly $130,000 a year. However, they rarely spent the entire salary, and some of them lived on $60,000 to $80,000 per year. Stanley and Danko were surprised to learn how many of these millionaires lived in modest homes, drove older cars, and avoided custom-tailored clothes and other ostentatious forms of consumption. And their reward? When asked, most expressed deep satisfaction about their financial security, while rejecting the costly luxuries which most people in lesser circumstances crave.

So, you also want to save, but don't want to be a miser. What are some painless ways to keep more of your modest income? My tax accountant advises his clients to pay off credit card debts immediately. The interest rates constitute highway robbery. Instead, take out a home equity loan or anything with a more reasonable rate. It's also possible to save a chunk on home or auto insurance by changing to a higher deductible. You need to contact your agent, since the resulting lower rates don't produce the same high profits for them. Other less obvious ways to save are cutting home utility costs by adjusting the thermostat and installing more insulation. If you require frequent medication, use generic drugs to save a bundle. Finally, bank, rather than spend, small windfalls such as income tax refunds.

Sometimes I'm asked whether it's possible to save too much. In rare cases, the answer could be yes. The U.S.

Congress, which writes our tax code, is toying with an "excess accumulation" tax on high IRA payouts. While tax policy is rather fluid, it is quite imaginable that lean times in the next century will force the government to raid tax-sheltered assets of wealthy individuals or their heirs. If you're one of the "heavy hitters" in the IRA category, you should check with your accountant about future tax consequences, and then possibly diversify your holdings.

Hobby Investing for Fun and Profit

The preceding section on fund investment applies to those who seek security and want to minimize risks. The plans we described involve basic decisions and then switching to "auto pilot" as the years go by and the funds accumulate. Once you feel safe, you might want to join those adventurous people who are starting to manage some of their own assets. As in many other fields, a little knowledge is a dangerous thing, and experts warn against wagering life savings in speculative ventures. Nevertheless, personal investing has become an enjoyable and lucrative hobby for many people. It also has elements of a game or sport, since the factor of risk constantly ping-pongs the "player" between the emotions of fear and greed. Some do it as lone wolves; others count on the collective wisdom of investment clubs, which have grown enormously over the past decades. Finally, personal investment is becoming a prime "do it yourself" occupation for management personnel who have been victims of corporate downsizing. With a computer and modem, this occupation can be pursued from a home, farm, or log cabin in the wild.

Personal investment requires both guts and knowledge. Besides the basic financial know-how, the fundamental skill involves recognizing a future need or demand ahead of others. The forecasts in Chapter 1, particularly as they pertain to demographic and technological developments, are a great starting point for sound investment strategies. Since we have a fairly good picture of the early 21st century world, let us identify the logical investment opportunities for today.

Follow the Boomers!

Marketing people are the most voracious consumers of demographic statistics. Usually, however, it involves a snapshot describing the population at any one time. We will concentrate on the large Baby Boom generation as it passes through life stages, creating and destroying markets as it goes. Correctly forecasting their needs will generate some truly phenomenal returns. Looking back, we note the dominant "youth culture" and markets of the 60s and 70s. As Boomers grow older, we recognize echos of this period in a wave of nostalgia, such as the popular "oldies" format on radio stations. But let's not dwell on the past, but consider the Boomers' future in terms of investment opportunities.

Nineteen ninety-six marked the year when the first members of this generation turned 50. Soon many more of them will reach this mid-life stage. Under normal circumstances, age 50 marks the peak earning years of a person's life. The housing situation is usually secure, and most child rearing obligations are met. Since Boomers have a reputation for not saving, this means that they will have a relatively large disposable income. This translates into more purchases of luxury items rather than necessities. Specifically, upscale cars, boats, entertainment, gourmet cuisine, resorts, and travel will be in demand. To get a picture, take a look at AARP's *Modern Maturity* magazine, particularly the advertisements. They depict mature people enjoying life to the fullest: collecting antiques, playing golf, and taking Caribbean Cruises. There is a particularly strong market for adventures that people may have missed in their earlier years. Hiking the Appalachian Trail, SCUBA diving, and other outdoor adventures are extremely popular with people who notice the aging process when looking in the mirror.

Aging, incidentally, is out. The most powerful investments are those for products and services which promise to keep Baby Boomers young. Necessity and fashion will conspire to make this the healthiest and most active older generation ever. Sports equipment and facilities which cater to the mature, upscale market will be in great demand. The same goes for medical and health-related services in the rejuvenation business. Plastic surgery, once available only to the rich and famous, will become commonplace as lasers and other mass-production techniques become widely available. Sexual appliances and stimulants will enjoy brisk sales. Various declining physical functions, which earlier generations took in stride, will be aggressively addressed. Pharmaceutical companies with remedies for hair loss, declining libido, arthritis, and other age-related problems stand to reap a fortune. Specialized clinics in the business of restoring youth and vigor have already started popping up. Don't be surprised when gland transplants, fetal sheep cell injections, and other daring treatments reach a shopping center near you.

The marriage of medicine and technology is now creating a rapidly expanding industry for human "spare parts." Many elderly people in the next century will become "bionic," with chunks of plastic, metal, and electronic gear in their bodies. Since the 70s, artificial joints have helped thousands escape disability. Now, artificial kidneys, pancreas, and other organs are on the way. Implantable micro-computers which aid vision, hearing, memory, and other sensory functions are in the advanced research stages. Meanwhile, other researchers are breeding animals to serve as organ and tissue donors for human beings.

Look for a boom in nutrition and dietary supplements. The food industry reports the greatest growth in products which claim health or weight-loss benefits. Meanwhile, there is a sales explosion in vitamins and other "dietary supplements" like minerals and herbal products. Although the U.S. Food and Drug

Administration frowns upon these nonprescription therapeutic preparations, health food merchants, selling "anti-aging" products, claim that the medical and pharmaceutical industries have conspired against them to maintain their profitable prescription monopoly. Have you tried Korean Ginseng, garlic tablets, or perhaps even Ginkgo Biloba, which is said to energize the mind?

Further down the road, as Baby Boomers reach their seventies and eighties, they will need to deal with more serious health problems and even disabilities. Investors with a long view will recognize a sharply-increased need for specialized medical facilities and equipment in the 2020s. Considering longer expected life spans and high costs of residential facilities, products, and services involving rehabilitation and home care will be particularly important. Gerontologists predict that the information age will also yield "assistive technologies" designed to allow a greater independence and autonomy in late life. Ultimately, of course, this generation must surrender its mortal life. This will give a boost to the funeral industry. By that time, cost and space considerations will have made conventional cemetery burial obsolete. Cremations will become routine, and the ashes will be stored in memorial urn vaults called columbariums.

Until then, comfort and security needs will dominate the elderly agenda. Housing, for instance, will be redesigned to allow even frail or disabled people freedom of motion and activity. Since labor costs are high, expect high levels of automation in future elder households. The same devices will make life more pleasant. Manufacturers are gearing up to produce electronic entertainment gear with sophisticated features to compensate for problems such as hearing or vision impairment. Auto designers are responding to the same imperatives. General Motors has actually brought some impaired individuals into the design process. GM learned that arthritis, which afflicts about 38 million Americans, creates real problems when elderly drivers try to turn a balky ignition switch. Designers are working to make all controls easier to see, reach, and manipulate. Ease of operation will be a major selling point for the auto industry in the next century.

Security is a related growth field. Whether real or imagined, concern with crime is still growing. The elderly are particularly vulnerable. Criminologists say that fewer young people in the future will translate into lower crime rates. Obviously, the crooks don't know about it yet. High youth unemployment may even boost crime in the future. Still, crime pays if you invest in the security industry. Privatization of government services was discussed in Chapter 2. The boom in corporate-owned prisons has just begun, and you may want to put some money into this "growth industry." Market analysts also predict strong sales for protective devices and services in the areas of loss control. As crime moves into the information age, everyone will need security devices to guard against "cyber-thieves" who can tap into your bank account with a few well-placed mouse clicks.

Aging, of course, is not the only future demographic change to interest investors. The other growth area is ethnic diversity. Hispanics and Asians, particularly, will constitute a much larger proportion of the population in the 21st century. Business has already begun to target products and services to the Spanish-speaking market in California, the Southwest, and Florida, which have high Latino population concentrations. As more of these people reach mainstream prosperity, investors would do well to anticipate their distinctive needs and economic clout.

Picking Technology Winners

While population patterns are quite predictable, technology trends are far more difficult to forecast over longer periods. The importance of the information age was discussed in Chapter 2. There will be both winners and losers in the technology sector.

Forecasting the dominant trends requires a fair amount of research and a little intuition. In many cases, future forecasts about the economy and demographic trends can be helpful. We know, for instance, that over time the economy will continue to be more capital intensive rather than labor intensive. One should certainly steer away from investing in industries which are falling behind in information age technology. Technology investors should also focus on demographic trends, particularly those where the needs of a changing population and technical innovation are destined to synergize.

Biotechnology is a classic example. Over the past decades, scientists have learned to manipulate the genetic make-up of living things ranging from microbes to farm animals. The immediate applications are in the areas of foods and medicines. Insulin, necessary for the treatment of diabetes, is now produced in vats of genetically-altered bacteria. Meanwhile, other bacteria are being "engineered" to consume harmful environmental toxins. It's hard to imagine how many new products and processes will come out of the laboratories of the 21st century.

The genetically-altered tomato, with a vine-ripened taste and long shelf life, has gotten the most public attention. There has been some backlash against altering Mother Nature, particularly when genetic manipulation enters the human realm. A lively debate has also arisen around the "ownership" of altered life forms. Nevertheless, this is a revolution which cannot be stopped. All of us should benefit enormously from improved food crops, medicines, and a host of other applications in the future. The fate of individual biotechnology companies is less clear. Industry experts advise investors to diversify their holdings or purchase mutual funds which specialize in this area.

Information technology, mentioned in the first chapter, will also continue to roll. Look for improved sophistication, power, and miniaturization in "thinking" machines. This translates into new applications and marriages with other technologies. Computers are almost completely wedded to communications and finance; applications in medical and biological sciences are following. Other fields, like law or agriculture, are still in the courtship stage. Experts recommend investments in these areas where pioneering applications are taking place. Don't forget that rapid advances also imply rapid obsolescence. The "Information Superhighway" is littered with the wreckage of once promising enterprises. Learn all you can before putting your money down.

A Daewoo in Your Future? Think Global!

Forecasters predict that the trend to global interdependence is far from complete. Investors need to keep an eye on foreign innovations and anticipate their impact on our domestic economy. Global investing offers some protection against speed bumps on Wall Street; on the other hand, it exposes investors to typical overseas risks such as political instability. Be cautious. Diversify. The NAFTA Treaty of the mid-90s was a signal that the U.S. intended to specialize in efficient, high-technology industries and leave low cost, labor-intensive operations to our Southern neighbor. It is hoped that Mexico will prosper and be able to purchase advanced American goods and services. Forecasters predict that the NAFTA free trade zone will ultimately move farther South to include regions of Central and South America. Canada, the other NAFTA partner, will continue to serve mainly as a source of raw materials and agricultural products, according to the opinion of U.S. economists.

Looking around the world, analysts note that investment opportunities in most of Latin America will likely remain mired by long-standing debt and corrupt politics. Europe, too, appears to be stagnant in the foreseeable future. That continent is also struggling with an aging population and overbuilt welfare state which will be a drag on the economy in the 21st century. An economic miracle in Russia and the former Soviet Union is too much of a long shot for most international economists. On the other hand, the experts are looking with eager anticipation at the Pacific rim countries of Asia. Everyone knows about Japan's success, but that's yesterday's news. After many years of spectacular growth, experts predict stagnation for the land of the rising sun.

Dynamic economic growth has also occurred in Taiwan, Singapore, Hong Kong, and Korea. The most daring forecasts say that China, or at least China's East Coast, will have the world's biggest economy within forty years. Viet Nam, India and other countries of that region are also said to have bright prospects over time.

South Korea offers a great example of both opportunities and risks in overseas investing. Throughout 1997, Korean borrowing got out of hand, and the International Monetary Fund had to step in with emergency loans to prevent a wave of bankruptcies. In fact, Korea's troubles were part of a domino effect triggered by economic jitters among Asian neighbors like Thailand and Honk Kong. Investors need to know that the market economies of these Asian countries are still in their infancy. Despite the potential for long-term growth, the ups and downs of the business cycle are far more pronounced than those of mature economies like ours. Business historians will tell you that America experienced spectacular booms and busts in the equivalent period of the 1800s. Since the "fundamentals" were sound, waves of failed investment (read speculation) did not harm the long-term growth of our economy.

The same thing probably applies to Korea as well. Bumps in the road? Sure. Patient investors should be aware that the fundamentals are good. After centuries in the shadow of powerful neighbors China and Japan, Korea is now hitting its stride. Reunification of North and South Korea will usher in a national renaissance. In the meantime, South Korea has built the world's most modern steel mill at Pohang to supply the robotic production line of Hyundai Motors. Hyundai became the world's tenth largest auto manufacturer in 1995. Other car makers, KIA and Daewoo, are also hitting the tough export market. And let's not forget that Korea is constructing its own version of Silicon Valley. It's worth noting that there are strong ties between Korea's political and economic leaders. Until 1995, foreigners were not permitted to purchase stock in the country's leading corporations. There will be excellent opportunities for investors as Korea begins to open its doors to outside capital and overcomes its fears of foreign control.

Korea is only one example of the opportunities for investors in the region. Other countries are also forging ahead in various sectors. Japan had to catch its breath after decades of wild economic expansion with a mild recession in the 90s. In the future, this country will pursue cutting-edge technologies, leaving more basic industrial processes to its neighbors. Nanotechnology is one example. This involves manipulating materials at the molecular and even atomic levels. The process is too complicated to explain here, but it implies shaping objects by precisely layering microscopic particles rather than taking a chunk of raw material and cutting it down to the desired shape. Once fully operational, innovations in this field could revolutionize the entire manufacturing world. Obviously, some of America's top scientists are working in this area as well.

Even though we focused principally on the United States in the opening chapter, other countries are experiencing some of the same changes. Europe is roughly equivalent to America in terms of economic and technological development. However, some newly industrialized countries of Asia are moving from traditional agricultural societies into the information age within the span of only a few decades. Traditional societies have more children, and birth control arrived much later there; thus, their social system has to play catch-up. For instance, Korea has had a centuries-old family-centered support system and only reluctantly adopted a form of Social Security in the 1990s. Japan has the world's longest life span and faces a very grave old-age support crisis in the next century. Charles Longino, demographer and gerontologist, notes a future economic paradox: Although America now imports products manufactured by young people in these countries, those workers will age in the 2030s and 2040s and will need to purchase the assistive technologies, goods, and services produced for America's aging Baby Boomers in the previous decades! What goes around comes around.

By the same token, America has much to learn from other countries. Visit Israel to see how households use solar energy as a substitute for electricity, or how drip irrigation solves the problem of water shortages in the desert. Meanwhile, Europeans are well ahead of us in terms of recycling to protect their environment. The continent is so densely populated that authorities have run out of unused space where wastes can be safely dumped. Besides recycling glass, paper, and scrap metal, governments are now asking manufacturers to create a closed cycle for their products. Germany is on the forefront; auto plants will be required to reclaim worn cars and reprocess all usable parts. In other words, no more junk yards. America is heading in the same direction. Major recycling will be employed for both environmental and economic reasons in the next century. Some firms are already doing it and not telling us. Have you seen the new "throw-away" cameras? Single use? Not so. One is led to believe that all but the film gets discarded. In truth, the mechanical parts are used over and over, and only the film and cardboard cover are replaced at the factory. Recycling and remanufacturing make good sense and will be an integral part of our 21st century economy. From this perspective, investing becomes an exciting adventure in exploring the future. We look beyond ourselves and see how our world is evolving. Knowledge is nothing if it is not paired with vision and imagination.

Chapter 5

TO YOUR HEALTH?: Corporate Medical Industry in an Aging America

An office visit in 2025: You've noticed a strange lump under your chin, a signal that there's something wrong. So you head for the clinic to get it checked out. On entering, signs direct you to a Diagnostic Center. It's basically a booth with a privacy curtain. Once inside, you're alone except for the glinting eye of a monitor camera in the corner. You are instructed to insert your left arm into an aperture and hardly notice how various robotic instruments measure your blood pressure, temperature, pulse, and draw minute amounts of blood which are analyzed simultaneously. By the way, the machine also verifies your identity and "reads" your medical history from a smart chip embedded in your arm. The chair you're sitting in is equipped to collect and analyze samples from the lower part of your body. While this is going on, you use your right hand to answer questions about your conditions on a touch-screen, using an anatomical model to point and click where it hurts. Then you head for the waiting room.

Within minutes, a specialized medical computer, called an "expert system," has digested the day's information and arrived at a diagnosis and treatment plan consistent with your medical history and physical condition. On the way out, another machine dispenses your prescription, a billing statement, and a patient's "advisory," describing your condition in layman's terms. The same machine records this information on the "smart chip" embedded in your arm. Doctors? Nurses? Yes, the clinic does have a skeleton staff of medical professionals to help folks with serious or complicated conditions. Incidentally, that lump under your chin turned out be an overgrown pimple, not a tumor.

If this scenario sounds farfetched, you should be aware that all of the technologies described above already exist in some fashion. Some leading medical schools currently use computerized "expert systems" to teach diagnostic skills, and medical authorities believe that the exploding volume of diagnostic information, pharmaceuticals, and other treatment options is about to overwhelm the memory of practicing physicians. The upcoming decades will witness the marriage of these robotic diagnostic devices with expert computers. At its logical conclusion, such functions as record keeping and financial and support services will be tied into the same system. But before describing future medical practice any further, a word on how we got there.

The last hundred years have surely witnessed an amazing transformation in health care. At the beginning of the 20th century, medicine was a combination of small business and philanthropy. Now it has become a virtual corporate enterprise tied to the government at various places. A new set of concepts using terms like capitation, formularies, and managed care are entering the medical vocabulary. While current and future developments are surely bewildering to the health care consumer, it all makes perfect sense in terms of the demographic, economic, and technological forecasts described at the beginning of this book. This chapter presents the evolution of the medical industry and how it will affect our lives and pocket books. Chapter 6 is devoted to more practical ideas on staying healthy without going broke in the next century.

Medicine, Science, and Technology

Until the end of the 19th century, doctors were very limited in what they could do for their patients. Except for some medication and a few primitive surgical procedures, physicians attempted to relieve suffering while nature took its course. The doctors themselves were independent tradesmen who had learned their craft through apprenticeship to established practitioners. Then came the modern medical school concept with a standardized, scientific curriculum. The early 20th century witnessed the gradual merging of medicine with other sciences, notably microbiology, chemistry, engineering, and electronics. Current techniques such as kidney dialysis hinged on the development of filter membranes, gastroenterology on the science of fiber optics, and brain scanning on advances in computer-imaging technology. As we head into the 21st century, genetic engineering and information-age technologies are taking center stage.

Ask your grandmother what happened when someone got sick in her younger days. Chances are she'll remember how the womenfolk tended the sick with chicken soup, hot compresses, and other home remedies. When things turned serious, the doctor was called. Most likely, the physician was a neighborhood hero and humanitarian, spending many sleepless nights at the bedside of his patients. Grandmother fondly remembers him for the care and devotion he offered the sick.

High-tech medicine has been both a blessing and a curse. Do you know anyone who has received an artificial knee or hip joint? Those procedures, like organ transplants, are true medical miracles and have helped enrich and prolong the lives of many people. On the other hand, as doctors became more like scientists, many patients complained that they had lost those values of care and compassion which mean so much to sick people. Although many sophisticated laboratory techniques rendered more accurate diagnoses, they had little influence on the ultimate outcome of a disease. The same can be said for intensive care technologies, which can usually keep a mortally-ill patient alive but rarely with the prospect of full recovery. Some techniques, such as electronic fetal monitoring, have even been accused of doing more harm than good. The final criticism is the extravagant expense of high tech medicine, especially for a society which has ignored low-cost preventive health care.

Doctors' Orders: The Strange World of Medical Economics

In the early part of this century, the typical physician had an office in his home and also took his little black bag to visit home-bound patients. He was a small businessman with a philanthropic flair, charging people what they could reasonably afford for his treatment and the medicine. Since most medical care was rendered at home, hospitals tended to be a charitable institution of last resort. Overall, people got the level of care they could afford, which unfortunately also meant that poor people received little or none at all. Yet, medical options were so limited that even wealthy people regarded it as a relatively minor consumer expense and did not spend a large portion of their income on health care. Today, the nation spends roughly 13 percent of its gross national income on a complex system of health care. That's roughly double the rate of what we spent in the late 60s, and the pace of increase is only now being contained. How did we get there?

At this point, a word about medical economics is in order. America has a free market economy, in which the consumer is king. Whether the product is real estate, groceries, or cars, savvy buyers shop around to find the best and most economical goods and services among a competing set of producers. Strong demand for superior goods drives up the prices, while oversupply and inferior products force prices down. Now, think of the doctor as supplier and the patient as consumer of health care. Except in rare cases, the provider determined both demand, what a patient needed, and the price of these services. Unlike the purchase of other goods, which involved consumer choice and some bargaining over price, the medical professionals made all decisions for the patient. Price competition, vital to the free market, was considered to be unethical within the tightly-knit professional community. The Hippocratic oath, you will recall, requires physicians to be "just and generous" with one another.

Until recently, this gave doctors a relatively free hand in determining a course of therapy. While professional guidelines such as peer review and second opinions had to be observed, the patient ultimately had to trust a physician's best judgment and pay the bill without questions. Moreover, standard medical practice and patient expectation pointed to the most aggressive, maximalist treatments which, according to prevailing medical culture, also required the most sophisticated, state-of-the-art equipment. Physicians' professional honor surely required no less.

From Black Bag Medicine to High-Tech Industry

This aggressive approach to medical practice was accelerated by two developments. One of them was the scientific revolution in medicine mentioned earlier. The other was a huge infusion of money from private health insurance and government programs in the latter half of the century. You will recall the economic boom of the postwar period. Besides pensions, businesses also granted health insurance to workers and their families. Most insurance plans were nearly openended, entrusting physicians and hospitals with a blank check for the subscribers' needs. The insurance companies, called "Third-Party Payers," effectively insulated both the patients and the medical establishment from the actual costs of medical services. Patients, particularly, got the mistaken impression that health care was "free."

As a result, the health care industry grew enormously in the 50s and 60s. Then, in 1965, the government entered the picture as an even bigger Third-Party Payer. In the context of the expanding Social Service programs of the period, Washington added the entitlements of Medicare and Medicaid. Medicare was intended mainly as a hospitalization program for elderly Social Security beneficiaries and was piggy-backed with a special tax on that popular program. Medicaid, on the other hand, was designed to provide medical, dental, and hospital benefits for indigent patients through a federal/state partnership.

The American Medical Association originally opposed both Medicare and Medicaid, thinking that this was the opening wedge of socialized medicine, where government would dictate the fees and destroy the hallowed sovereignty of the medical profession. The Congress, however, kept the existing "fee for service" billing mechanism intact, turning the twin afflictions of poverty and ill health into a bonanza for the health care industry. Even welfare recipients and retirees, who had earlier been denied access to the system following unfavorable wallet biopsies, now became eligible for costly, high-tech medicine. Physicians and hospitals, meanwhile, saw not only patients but blank checks from the government permitting them to expand services and facilities. For many, it was an invitation to over-billing and fraud. The only losers were the taxpayers.

Within the span of a few years, health care became one of the most profitable industries. Hospitals were transformed from dingy, charitable institutions into gleaming temples of corporate healing technologies. Doctors were lured to practice there with the promise of the finest facilities, not to mention a host of fringe benefits.

The competition for doctors and patients assumed near "arms race" proportions Each hospital tried to outdo others in terms of big ticket items such as magnetic scanners, lithotripters, etc., while pampering patients with luxurious amenities rivaling high-class hotels and cruise ships. Naturally, hospitals and physicians, who had invested in new equipment and facilities, could be compensated only by maximum usage. This explains how supply created demand, turning Adam Smith's rules of free market economics on their heads! The patients had no role in this but to follow doctors' orders while the mountains of bills went directly to insurance companies and the federal treasury.

Patients did get involved in medical finances when things went wrong in the course of a treatment; opportunistic lawyers goaded them into demanding large malpractice settlements. The doctors responded with "defensive medicine," going well beyond the normal limits on costly diagnostic tests and therapeutic procedures to protect themselves against potentially devastating malpractice suits.

How Much Health Care is Enough?

While the U.S. population has grown only modestly in recent decades, medical spending from both public and private sources is skyrocketing. The numbers themselves are stunning; consider that outlays increased more than tenfold from 1965 to 1980, and that total dollar amounts, once calculated in billions, are now hitting the trillions. The knee-jerk reaction might be to blame greedy doctors and hospitals, but that is only a small part of the story. The large number of people who suddenly became eligible for care and the intensity and variety of care played a much larger role. What happened, essentially, is that, besides growth of private insurance, large sectors of the population had become eligible for "socialized," or government-sponsored medicine. That included the elderly, welfare recipients, the armed forces, and, last but not least, members of Congress with their access to military hospitals. The only uninsured group turned out to be the "working poor," who were not covered by employer insurance plans, but who earned too much to receive Medicaid.

For the most part, eligible recipients received the finest, most advanced health care in the world, and their medical bills seemed to prove it. Under the "fee for service" policy, doctors and other health care providers were at liberty to bill for any service they considered appropriate. Fees were set on a "customary" basis, essentially an unwritten gentlemens' agreement within the medical community. The system was virtually open-ended, with neither incentives nor controls on medical costs. Since hospital stays were eligible for highest levels of reimbursement, doctors and hospital authorities routinely admitted far too many patients. Diagnostic and laboratory services were also overused. To be sure, some unethical doctors and other health care providers milked, and sometimes even defrauded, the system for their personal benefit. In all likelihood, a number of procedures, like routine tonsillectomies, hysterectomies, and cardiac bypass surgery, may have been more beneficial for the surgeon than the patients. The resulting ten-fold increase in costs certainly did not translate into a ten-fold improvement of the nation's health status.

Actually, Americans also got a larger variety of care. Besides doctor and hospital care, we also learned to appreciate the host of other related services provided by podiatrists, chiropractors, and physical therapists, to name only a few. Afflictions like mental and emotional illness, drug and alcohol abuse, which in the past had caused a lot of silent suffering, now also came within the realm of medical treatment and insurance reimbursement. Contemporary Americans have come to expect a lot from their health care system, at least more than previous generations. From this perspective, much of the expense may ultimately be justified. Everything else has gone up in price, and health may be a far more worthwhile national expense than casino gambling or many other activities that empty our wallets.

Who'll Pay the Bill?

The costly expansion of the medical industry collided with unfavorable economic and demographic forces in the 1980s and 1990s. As discussed in Chapter 1, the economy began to slow down in the 70s, and with the arrival of the information age, began to shake out excess personnel. The corporate downsizing movement, described in Chapter 2, called not only for dismissal of excess personnel but also for eliminating or trimming fringe benefits. Besides pensions, health insurance was an easy target. Health care costs had risen much faster than other employee expenses, jumping nearly 20 percent annually for the average company. Figure 1 shows the evolving relation between wages and health care costs. When adjusted for inflation, salaries remained steady, while medical costs rose steeply. You probably thought the boss was a tightwad when examining the "take home" portion of your pay stub; the boss, meanwhile, was grinding his teeth about the company's ever-growing health insurance bill. It is said that the major U.S. auto builders were now paying more for employee health care than the steel used to manufacture their vehicles! Corporations were desperate to trim these costs for current employees and retirees who had also been guaranteed a health plan. It also accounts for rising overtime in American industry. Workers need time off, but the employers want to boost output without hiring additional personnel who might be eligible for these costly fringe benefits.

Our government's situation was not much different. While Medicaid posed a problem, the greatest crisis loomed in the Medicare area. Figure 2 shows Congressional estimates of future expenses. It is a steeply rising curve. Like the related

Health Care Benefits Compared to Wages
Percentage Increase From 1965 to 1991

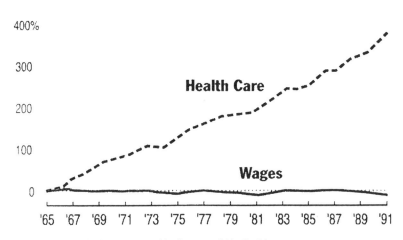

* Adjusted for inflation; includes Medicare and Medicaid

Source: Health Care Financing Administration

Projected Growth of Medicare Spending
(Billions of Dollars)

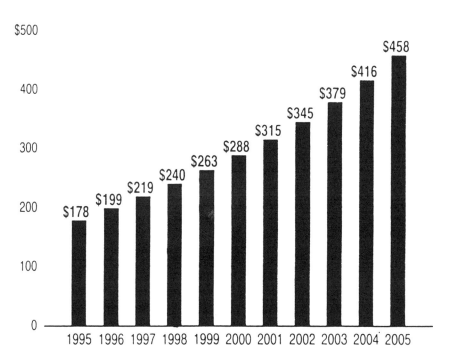

Source: Congressional Budget Office, April 1995

Social Security fund, Medicare depended on taxes from working people. The declining dependency ratio of fewer contributing workers spelled trouble in the long run. In fact, the authorities discovered that a total Medicaid spend-down was likely in the first few years of the new millennium! These calculations were based on rising medical costs combined with the rapidly growing number of retirees who would need care for the remainder of their enhanced life span. At that point, "saving medicare" turned into a major fear monger issue in the politics of the late nineties. No one, it seemed, wanted to give up any future benefits or pay more taxes.

The Battle of Cost Control

Health care experts have identified three major approaches to cost reduction. All of them involve rationing for patients and controls on health care providers. The first, and most drastic, is a National Health Care system, modeled on programs in Canada and Great Britain. Everyone would be covered, and cost would come out of general government revenues. Savings would be achieved because a single payer, the government, would eliminate the middleman profits and paperwork of the commercial insurance industry. Such a system was proposed by the Clinton administration in 1993, but it was shot down in a Conservative Congress after violent protests from the medical and insurance industries. They presented it as an ideological argument against Socialism; government would become a health care dictator, depriving people of free choice in medical care. Actually, it would have been more like an extension of existing Medicare/Medicaid programs to the general population. Besides, most people don't have that many choices anyway.

If you ever meet a Canadian, ask about his health care system. It seems to have both strengths and weaknesses. Government officials are proud that overall costs have been held in check. Figure 3 compares Canada to the U.S. in terms of proportional spending. Ordinary Canadians, however, are quite critical. Yes, the medical establishment does a good job with preventive care and routine care for simple ailments, but it is difficult to get a serious operation or other high-cost therapy. It seems that the government's rationing policy operates by making access very difficult. Some seriously-ill patients worry whether they will survive while waiting in line. A desperate few, who can afford it, head south and get operations at their own expense in the United States. Despite these shortcomings, none of these Canadians would be willing to trade their system for ours.

State and federal regulation of the medical industry is another approach to curbing costs. Favored by Liberals, it assumes that medical prices are set by providers rather than free market competitive forces. Did you know that medical fees are highest in communities served by a large number of doctors and hospitals? If a large number of providers competes for a small pool of patients, they must jack up the prices and utilization of medical services to survive. Yes, hospitals and doctors do compete, but rarely on the basis of price. "Certificates of Need" are a typical example of government regulation here. Before a hospital can expand or purchase a large item of equipment, it must first be determined that the new acquisition will not duplicate existing facilities in the community. Prospective payment for medical procedures is another regulatory device. Using a standard set of specific ailments called Diagnostic Related Groups (DRG), the government, insurance company, or other payer agrees to reimburse doctors and hospitals specific fees for treating each case.

Currently there are roughly 476 DRGs in the country, covering everything from broken bones to brain tumors. The standard fees are set on the skimpy side to encourage cost control. To be sure, providers can only come out ahead if they stay under the limits consistently. Reducing the number of days in the hospital is a critical factor, and any hospitalized patient will

Figure 3

U.S. - Canadian Cost Comparison

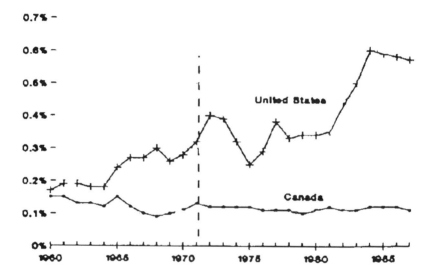

***Costs of Health Insurance and Administration as
Percent of Gross National Product***

tell you about the rush to get him out. Another tool of standardization and cost control is Professional Standards Review Organizations (PSROs). These government-mandated peer review organizations audit treatment records for quality and cost effectiveness. Obviously, individual doctors are losing much of their autonomy in the process.

The final cost control strategy, which is discussed in the next section, involves a concept called "managed competition." The object is to structure doctors, hospitals, and other providers into companies called Health Maintenance Organizations, HMOs. They provide a complete package of health care for a set monthly fee. It is also called "prepaid care," and the individual's share is referred to as "capitation." Patients like the idea of modest, predictable medical expenses without the bothersome paperwork. HMOs can earn a profit when these fees exceed actual treatment expenses. Thus, HMOs give the doctors an incentive to keep group members healthy and then use the most cost-effective treatment should they become ill. When there are a number of HMOs in a community, they will compete for patients on the basis of monthly fee and reputation for quality. Despite a number of problems, this model, plus a number of features from the other cost-control techniques, is destined to dominate the American medical landscape for years to come. Figure 4 traces the rapid growth of this phenomenon. As with many other trends, California led the way, and other states are rapidly getting on the bandwagon. It is a system which most government officials, particularly Conservatives, heartily endorse.

Understanding Managed Care

For many of us, managed care is a lot like the computer. You may resist it, you may not be able to understand it, but, like it or not, it's here to stay. Take the case of Sandra, one of our neighbors. Late every spring Sandra starts gagging and wheezing, all the classic signs of severe allergic reaction to various blooming plants. But Sandra knows what to do. She heads to the

Managed Care

Enrollment in Health Maintenance
Organizations (HMOs), In Millions

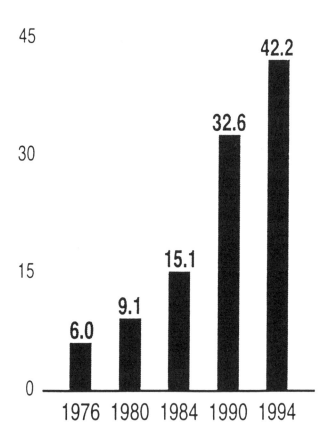

Source: U.S. Department of Health and Human
Services

allergist who prescribes a medicine so familiar that she has memorized its name. This familiar pattern was broken when her husband's company switched to an HMO to cut down on medical costs. Sandra is furious; she can no longer go straight to the allergy specialist; he's not even on the HMO's list. Instead, she must first report to a nurse and endure a general practitioner's exam when she well knows her problem. All of this seems like a terrible waste of time for Sandra. If she is lucky, the HMO will eventually allow her a limited number of visits with their allergist. By the way, it's tough to get an appointment with a specialist. Hay fever season will be over when you finally get there. The final insult, she'll tell you, comes when the specialist refuses to write her familiar prescription, saying it isn't part of the HMO formulary. Well, then, how about that great new allergy medicine featured in full-page ads of the current *Parade* magazine? Sorry, you'll have to pay for that yourself.

Like many of us, Sandra discovered that the concept of managed care represents medicine's transition from a healing art to a corporate enterprise. It is also a code word for rationing, since each patient's treatment has a budget not to be exceeded. On the other hand, the HMOs which practice managed care offer their members distinct advantages. By having a judicious system of rationing, they keep premiums reasonable. In most cases consumers have a choice of HMOs or similar systems. After joining, the choices decline as most patients are assigned a doctor, or "preferred provider," as the insurance companies like to call them. Another benefit is that the HMO covers all illnesses, even those where extended hospital stays could bankrupt a normal family. Finally, HMOs focus on preventive care, insisting on immunizations, physical examinations, and healthy lifestyles, which can head off more serious and costly ailments in the long run.

The problems with HMOs and managed care are that the providers and insurers are ultimately guided by the corporate goals of profit rather than intrinsic needs of their patients. To begin with, they tend to engage in "cherry picking," preferring to serve young and healthy segments of the population. Since elderly and disabled people usually account for higher costs, one HMO deliberately located its admission department at the top of a steep stairwell to screen out physically-challenged individuals. Some HMOs also place "lifetime" limits on certain services, such as hospitalization for mental illness.

In addition, there are subtle barriers to utilization. The most obvious one is the difficulty of getting doctors' appointments. Clinic managers go under the assumption that if health care is "free," people will show up with every little ache and pain which will likely have disappeared by the next morning anyway. It can be a major annoyance. A small co-payment for each visit or drug prescription also discourages frivolous patient visits. Once there, patients are "triaged," or screened by a nurse, to determine whether a physician is really needed. All treatments must be initiated by a general practitioner, nowadays called a family medicine or primary care physician. He or she, incidentally, is the lowest paid member of the profession. Visits to specialists, who demand higher fees, require permission of the patient's primary care physician. Even then, the options are limited, because elite doctors within many communities choose not to participate in a provider "network" fed by minimal fees.

Other cost-control measures test a physician's professional ethics. Doctors are aware that their salaries are ultimately tied to the profitability of the HMO. They are directed to hold costs down by all possible means. Periodically, irate patients learn that doctors operate under clandestine "quotas" which limit expensive operations and therapies. Some patients are reduced to begging for treatments the HMO is reluctant to fund. The doctors themselves have rebelled against "gag rules," which prohibit them from discussing effective but expensive treatment options with their patients. Fortunately, most HMOs are not so predatory and do operate in an ethical manner. Nevertheless, the traditional confidential relationship between doctor and patient is slowly giving way to the suspicion and mistrust found in the business world.

Finally, we should mention how HMOs dispense prescription drugs. The concept of managed care is embodied in "Formularies," a term used to describe a standard set of drugs judged to be both effective and reasonably priced. HMOs and hospitals buy their formulary stocks in bulk from pharmaceutical manufacturers after hard bargaining. It explains, by the way, why independent pharmacies are going out of business. They and their customers simply don't have the bargaining power of the health care conglomerates.

Have you wondered why drug manufacturers recently began multi-million dollar TV and magazine advertising campaigns for prescription drugs? You can't buy them without a doctor's prescription. So why the hard sell? Typically, new drugs are the most expensive and least likely to find their way into the formularies. The pharmaceutical companies hope that these ads will influence patients to put pressure on doctors or even pay for these upscale prescriptions out of their own pockets. It seems that cost controls put a squeeze on just about everyone!

Do you enjoy one-stop shopping? In the interest of efficiency, future health care organizations will consolidate various functions in the same way chain supermarkets absorbed local bakers, fruit stands, and butcher shops, not to mention the corner drugstore. Most significantly, these conglomerates will also merge the provider with insurance functions since HMOs already constitute de facto health insurance! You could say that money will be saved by elimininating the insurance "middleman" between patient and provider. Looking even further into the future, forecasters envision the merger of these functions with business corporations or government agencies. They're the ones who have the greatest motivation for cost control and would surely like to bring these operations under their roof. While this poses threats to the privacy of patients and autonomy of health professionals, the imperative of efficiency will surely win out. Major industries already have in-house "occupational health" medical staffs.

They'll try to sell you on the convenience of it all. Yet, it's a mixed blessing for the health care consumer of the next century. On the one hand, the streamlined system will be both efficient and economical; on the other hand, individuals will face monolithic giants with few choices or authorities to turn to if things go wrong. Imagine yourself as a worker at a chemical plant. Do the periodic check-ups by the occupational health nurse serve your well-being or the liability status of the corporation? Privacy will also suffer. Do you really want supervisors to have access to your medical records? More about this in the next chapter.

Medical Occupations in Transition

If you're a medical professional and think you're safe from the demographic, economic, and technological trends described in earlier chapters, you're dead wrong. Physicians, the kingpins of our health care system, are in for a demotion of sorts. Traditional medicine gave doctors almost total autonomy. They were both practitioners of the healing art and independent business people. Within future managed care conglomerates, physicians will assume the role of employees, subject to management decisions made by medical business executives. Private medical practice is about to disappear; frankly, many physicians are happy to trade "paperwork" responsibilities of a small business for the regular hours and predictable paychecks offered by an HMO. Group practices, where a number of physicians share facilities and administrative services, are an intermediate step in this consolidation. Only eccentric doctors operating "boutique" practices featuring unconventional and elective treatments like acupuncture, baldness cures, and sex change operations are likely to escape medical merger mania.

Next, expect to see fewer specialists. Earlier in this century, most physicians were general practitioners. Then, with the introduction of many new technologies and branches of medicine, the specialists seized the professional high ground. Now, believe it or not, the generalists are back in demand. The reason is cost control. Until recently, most insurance companies gave patients carte blanche when selecting a physician. After a quick self diagnosis, most folks headed straight for a specialist. Since specialties generate higher income, more and more doctors chose this route as well. It turned out that affluent urban areas became saturated with medical specialists who could make a living only by charging higher prices to fewer patients, often performing services well below their skill levels. From this perspective, America actually seemed to be oversupplied with physicians. In fact, there has been an imbalance. Poorer and rural regions of the country have had a shortage of doctors. Wealthy, urban areas have had an excess, particularly of overqualified specialists. Managed care will shift this distribution in favor of general practice. To maintain their income, many specialists are turning to elective procedures, such as cosmetic plastic surgery, for private patients with deep pockets.

Other medical professionals, who work with doctors, can also expect change. Even the casual clinic visitor will note that many tasks have been reassigned. For instance, so called "para-professionals" like physicians' assistants and nurse practioners are taking over some duties from medical doctors. Psychiatrists know that once psychologists are allowed to prescribe psycho-active medications, their specialty, based on lengthy Freudian analysis, will quickly disappear. Some say it already has. Meanwhile, registered nurses are being supplanted by licensed practical nurses, and so on. This saves salary costs and makes great sense from a management standpoint. Will care suffer? Defenders of managed care say that overqualified medical staffs are a waste; besides, the system has many built-in supervision and review procedures. As the number of highly paid professionals declines, technical and administrative staffs will grow. Nevertheless, computers and information technology are rapidly replacing people in such areas as medical records, financial operations, and laboratories.

The relationship between medical personnel and technology innovations, like lasers and computers, has been a curious one. Initially, each new technology also spawned new medical specialties. Physicians had to essentially immerse themselves into the new technologies. Unlike other industries, where technologies typically led to labor-saving automation, those in the medical field actually boosted the number of highly-specialized physicians. Two things have happened since then. First, cost control measures like managed care and Certificates of Need curbed reckless technology diffusion; in addition, second and third generations of high-tech equipment have become more "user friendly."Procedures like laser surgery, which once required a doctor to become part physicist, now can be learned in weekend seminars. Overall, information age technology promises to make health care professionals far more capable and efficient in the future.

Let's not forget the international dimension. Chapter One discussed economic globalization. In terms of worker mobility, America has become a magnet for physicians from other countries. Many of them have been trained in Third World countries, typically Asia, and seek a better life on our shores. Others received training in U.S. medical schools, as a form of foreign aid, but then chose to stay here for the same reasons. The American Medical Association, speaking for U.S. doctors, has complained that these foreign doctors are creating a glut in the profession, reducing the opportunities for American physicians. On the other hand, many of these foreigners have filled the low-pay, long-hour intern positions at overcrowded inner city hospitals which serve minorities and indigent patients. If you'd like to meet an Indian or Pakistani, visit the emergency room of your local public hospital. Believe me, they're appreciated!

Medical Practice in the Future

It's now obvious why private practice physicians and charitable community hospitals are being swept away by corporate medical conglomerates organized along industrial lines for efficiency and profit. Actually, traditional medical practice is already an anachronism and is finally catching up with the main-stream economy. After all, stores, restaurants, auto service shops, and nearly all other businesses operate on a large scale and are organized into regional, national, and even international chains. All operations, including advertising, inventory, and personnel management, are much more efficient on a large scale. Ask any graduate of McDonald's "Hamburger University."

Now it's health care's turn for the corporate make-over. To begin with, medical practices will be rearranged for maximum efficiency. That means being able to treat large numbers of patients in a process or assembly line fashion. Visualize, if you can, the transition from a workshop to a factory and then add automation as described at the beginning of the chapter. Efficiency is further enhanced by placing supportive services like X-rays, laboratories, and pharmacies under the same roof. This saves everyone, including patients, a lot of running around. Other savings can be achieved by buying medical supplies, like pharmacy formularies, in bulk. Since hospital facilities are so expensive, the "hotel" role will be eliminated by performing most surgeries on an "out-patient" basis. As a matter of fact, health care analysts predict the demise of the traditional hospital, where short-term and long-term patients were bedded together. You can expect three distinct facilities: one offering "drive-through" clinics for otherwise healthy patients; intensive care wards for those who are incapacitated and in a critical condition. A third facility for chronically ill patients, usually called a nursing home, will be discussed in the next section.

Finally, corporate management decisions will steer the future of health care enterprises. Almost everything we have witnessed in the business world will happen here. This includes mergers and consolidations, with conglomerates struggling for market share for their hospitals and other health-related facilities. Some medical professionals, like nurses and clinic workers, notice the pressure to downsize staffs and achieve savings through personnel reductions. There is talk that the once autonomous doctors are even thinking of forming a union! This concern for the bottom line will anger many people who have always thought of medical care as a public service. Unprofitable locations, like inner cities or remote rural areas, have the most to fear. Ideally, a physician's assistant, located in the wild, will be able to reach a "telecommuting" doctor for diagnosis and treatment via data links. The concept of managed care competition may be efficient but not necessarily the most caring from the patient's point of view.

Baby Boomers, Medicare, and the Long-Term Care Dilemma

If your family is typical, adult children spend a fair amount of time contemplating their aging parents' future. Those of us who are responsible create vivid scenarios of what might happen to Mom or Dad and how this will affect our own lives. Do you dread getting the bills and writing their checks? A stroke or a terminal cancer diagnosis tends to come when we are least prepared for it, say during a business trip or vacation. The elders typically shake it off, preferring not to dwell on their personal decline and demise. Who can blame them? But you, the middle-aged adult, are close to becoming their "parent" and assuming responsibility for their affairs during the remainder of their lives. Serious decisions will have to be made, but how much help can you expect?

The storm signals are up as health care experts desperately warn the nation about Medicare's crash in the first years of the 21st century. Medicaid is nearly as shaky. While politicians are making hay by scaring the public and blaming each other, you won't find any real villains here. Demographics, generous entitlements, and expansion of the health care system are at the root of the problem. Social Security, discussed in Chapter 3, can no longer support the promise and expectation of our mid-century expansion into the next millennium.

Here's the problem. No one really foresaw the eventual aging of the Baby Boomers, nor the arrival of the information age, which would alter the traditional work force. Even the longevity of the current crop of senior citizens was underestimated. In terms of numbers, the percentage of elderly people in the population is steadily rising. According to census figures, those over 65 accounted for 13 percent of the population in the mid-90s, but that percentage is expected to double within 30 years. The proportion of extremely old people, those over 85, is climbing even faster. Meanwhile, elderly people, particularly the very old, consume medical resources at a much higher rate than the rest of the population. Hospital statistics indicate that, in terms of a lifetime, people typically consume the most health care dollars during the last weeks of their existence. Rarely, if ever, does an individual's Medicare tax contributions cover these costs. Typically, doctors attempt intense, but futile, efforts to hold onto life with any available technological means. If you want to experience real sticker shock, have someone show you a hospital bill which involved a stay in an Intensive Care Unit. While this is a costly death, consider the financial circumstances of elderly people who have become disabled by Alzheimer's, Parkinson's, and other diseases. They need nursing home care, which currently averages over $40,000 a year. Thanks to increases in longevity, not to mention inflation, the current and future bills for these patients are and will be enormous, and could be a crushing burden to Baby Busters in the next century. So, what can we do?

Paying the Bill

Government budget experts are currently trying to figure out ways by which everyone can be cared for without a fiscal melt-down. In practical terms this means that future government policies will be designed to persuade individuals to cover the lion's share of their medical expenses, with public assistance available only as a last resort for those who have no other resources. Under no circumstances should public money be spent for the care of people who are not destitute. As you can imagine, this is going to be a hard sell for those of us who thought that our Medicare tax contributions would insulate us from late life medical costs. That, unfortunately, is the bottom line.

There are a number of specific proposals to slay the dragon of old-age health care costs. The most extreme proposals came from the Americans for Generational Equity and some physicians. Richard Lamm, a former governor of Colorado, achieved national notoriety in 1984 by suggesting that terminally ill elders have "a duty to die and get out of the way with all our machines and artificial hearts and everything else like that and let the other society, our kids, have a reasonable life." If the situation continues, Lamm calculates that today's generation of children will have to subsidize each current retiree to the tune of $100,000 for old-age health care. Lamm's solution lies in scaling back extreme measures for dying patients. "No other nation in the world would take a 90-year-old with congestive heart failure out of a nursing home and put him into an intensive care unit," says Lamm according to a recent *Newsweek* quote. Lamm also proposes to cut off millionaires, 20 percent of whom currently get Medicare. Actually, all wealthy people should be subject to a "means test" prior to receiving public benefits. Lamm would likewise shake well-to-do people off the Social Security rolls and severely curtail military retirement pay for the same group. Needy folks would continue to receive judiciously-determined benefits.

Another way of cutting costs is to reduce the fees of doctors and hospitals for treating Medicare and Medicaid patients. That's dangerous, however. Some physicians are refusing patients in this category or demanding extra fees for treatment. Some Medicare patients can afford supplemental insurance to cover the difference. However, it defeats the program's goal of universal accessibility.

Fans of the managed competition concept are pushing the idea of Medicare HMOs. Although it's probably inevitable, the initiative is meeting some resistance. HMOs favor healthy clients and fear bankruptcy if they must cater to an elderly population. The elderly don't like the idea of giving up their choice of physician, and fear they will be short-changed within a managed care system. Nevertheless, this would be a way to save administrative expenses and other costs. In the long run, Medicare HMOs will probably become mandatory.

Extended nursing home care presents the greatest long-range problem. We know that Medicare covers only acute, short-term illnesses, but not the chronic, long-term afflictions which are usually incurable. Medicare permits only brief nursing home stays, which may be unavoidable in these cases. What happens then is the so-called "spend-down" mentioned in Chapter 3. Patients must draw on their own resources until they are nearly exhausted. Considering the expense, this could happen rather quickly. They would then become eligible for Medicaid, since it is designed for indigent individuals. Roughly 50 percent of all nursing home bills are currently covered by Medicaid.

While everyone favors cost-cutting, the money will have to come from somewhere. The most draconian proposals, perhaps, are "filial responsibility" laws, by which states seek to recover Medicaid expenditures from deceased patients' estates and even the assets of surviving relatives. As you can imagine, this is not a popular idea. Another track is to use alternatives such as adult day care or home health care for those patients who do not need to be institutionalized. Figure 5 offers an expert projection of residential arrangements for disabled senior citizens. Under most circumstances, the elderly prefer to stay at home and receive periodic visits from a nurse or housekeeping aide, but this also causes problems. There may not be a family care giver, and many women, who have traditionally filled this role, cannot afford to leave the work force. They would have to be paid. Although this makes sense, medical personnel contend that family members don't have the requisite training and may exploit the patient's disability to their own benefit.

Another approach would be to give up the fiction that everyone pays for his or her own health care. This would involve tapping the general fund and taxing everyone to subsidize those in need. Not so long ago, a proposal was made in Congress stating that bills for people with potentially bankrupting, or "catastrophic" illnesses, be supported with a 15 percent surtax on the taxable income of retired people. Even though leaders of the AARP supported the idea, the vast majority of its membership and other elderly rejected this enlightened idea and had the legislation killed.

Would you like to avoid ever having to depend on someone else in case of disability? Do you need another tax shelter? Recently, insurance companies started offering Long Term Care (LTC) insurance to cover nursing home expenses. There have been few takers. The premiums are prohibitive; only a wealthy person, with a sizeable inheritance to protect, could afford this coverage. Now, however, the government is getting into the act, offering tax write-offs to the insured. Anything to reduce the nation's future Medicare burden makes good sense.

The best solutions, no doubt, involve reducing the number of people who need this type of care. People should exercise the voluntary option of adjusting their lifestyles to stay healthy for longer periods of their lives. To some degree, this is already happening and will be discussed more fully in the next chapter. To help this process along, government should perhaps also divert more funds to research in wellness and prevention for the elderly. As of this writing, the National Institutes of Health spend only about six percent of their research money on age-related problems. For

Figure 5

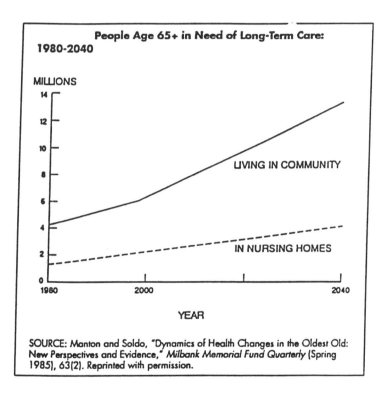

People Age 65+ in Need of Long-Term Care: 1980-2040

LIVING IN COMMUNITY

IN NURSING HOMES

SOURCE: Manton and Soldo, "Dynamics of Health Changes in the Oldest Old: New Perspectives and Evidence," *Milbank Memorial Fund Quarterly* (Spring 1985), 63(2). Reprinted with permission.

example, osteoporosis, a weakening of the bones, often leads to hip fractures, followed by permanent disability. Only small advances in treatment would save millions in hospitalization and nursing home stays for many potential victims. Other research in prevention and cures for Alzheimer's, cardiovascular ailments, stroke, arthritis, and the like could pay vast dividends in terms of healthy old folks and reduced institutionalization in the next century.

Look for National Health Care to Return

Health care analysts predict that more and more people will overspend their public entitlements and personal savings during the last phase of their lives in the next century. Since this forecast is totally credible and will affect all members of society, a public financing solution will have to be found. The tragedy, perhaps, is that action will not come until there is a genuine, unavoidable national crisis. It's closer than we think, and it will involve a reordering of our values as well. Specifically, we will need to rethink whether health care is a public or private commodity. In the past, medical care was a private purchase, governed by the needs and resources of individual patients. Yet, in the last half century, cooperative and public financing have become the norm. Nowadays, almost everyone believes that good health is an important national resource which deserves public support even if it smells of collectivism.

The end result, no doubt, will be a two-tier system reflecting our concern for the needy while preserving traditional American values of choice and individualism. A lower tier will be created by merging Medicare and Medicaid with Veterans and Military Health systems plus other public medical facilities. It will provide austere, necessary medical services to everyone who could not otherwise afford it. Meanwhile, the more traditional insurance system will offer a large variety of optional health services for those with deeper pockets. So, imagine a future "health cafeteria" where everyone is entitled to the life-sustaining main course, but the trimmings, such as elective surgery, are optional. It's a solution we can both live with and afford.

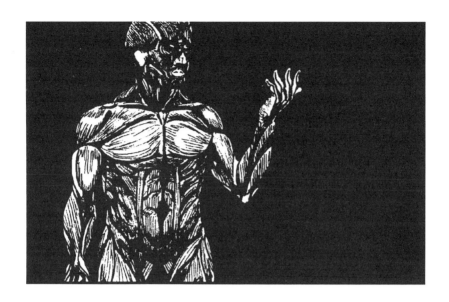

Chapter 6

BE YOUR OWN DOCTOR:
You Do Have Choices!

If your work place is like mine, medical issues often dominate coffee break chatter. Women compare hysterectomies, while men trade cholesterol counts. There are tales of operations, drug intolerance, and eye-popping anesthesia bills. Jerry, an accountant, entertains colleagues with harrowing stories of his recent quadruple by-pass surgery. Did you know that they cut blood vessels from your legs to replace sections of the heart's plumbing system? Once Jerry leaves the room, the talk quickly turns to how he got that way. By all accounts, Jerry was a chain smoker who feasted on greasy foods and avoided all types of exercise except shouting at subordinates. The rest of us knew that this lifestyle made him a candidate for heart disease, but we were too polite to tell him so. Or maybe we were afraid of his fiery temper. Had Jerry paid more attention to his health, he probably would not have needed so much expensive and painful health care.

The preceding chapter predicted problems for the health care industry, but that doesn't mean your personal health status is hopeless. Actually, you have more power over your health than over your career, investments, and financial fate. Health is also your most valuable personal asset. It's something that individuals can achieve and manage under normal circumstances. When it fails, medical care is required. All too often our society has mistakenly equated health care with health. Folks like Jerry look at their bodies as they do the family car which breaks down from time to time. The doctor, as any good mechanic, then cuts it open and fixes or replaces the parts. Curiously, we provide oil changes, tire rotations, and other maintenance services for our cars; our bodies, meanwhile, receive so little preventive care! This chapter tells what we must do for ourselves. Let's begin by learning how to navigate the medical system.

You, the Health Care Consumer

Have you ever thought of yourself as a consumer of medical services? If not, it's about time. To be sure, the managed care system described in the last chapter cries out for informed, emancipated patients. The basic incentive for HMOs and similar providers is to turn a profit. Meanwhile, "gag rules" prevent doctors from telling the whole truth about preferred therapies, while formularies restrict costly drug regimes. In earlier times, the conventional wisdom was to trust your doctor. At least that's what Dear Abby and Ann Landers told their readers. Nowadays, with profit-oriented managed care incentives, you can't be sure he's on your side. So what do you do?

As with any other important matter, the first step involves self-education. As the trust relationship between doctors and patients erodes, more and more people seek information about diseases and treatments on their own. Medical texts written for the layman fill libraries and book stores. Medical schools at major universities like Harvard and Johns Hopkins publish "Health Letters," detailing the latest news in various fields of medicine for their subscribers. Meanwhile, news magazines regularly feature health news, interspersed by those ubiquitous "Ask Your Doctor About...." pharmaceutical ads. Some of it may be phony, misleading, or disguised advertising. Still, there's more than enough competent medical information available. As you can imagine, doctors are not always enthusiastic about this, since it punctures some of the mystique which surrounds their profession. Most would prefer a passive patient, fearful that a little learning is a dangerous thing. Nevertheless, the informed medical consumer, who knows the range of options, receives more respect and is far more likely to get what he or she needs.

Possibly the most important choice is that of selecting an HMO or other managed health care plan. Although the idea was conceived with "choice" in mind, few people know what to look for or what questions to ask. This is where some knowledge really pays off. A prospective patient should look over the list of physicians and other professional personnel who work there. What specialties are represented? Are they Board Certified? With which hospitals are they affiliated? These are some worthwhile questions. Probing deeper, the medical consumer should also ask about the financial status of the organization, limits and exclusions of medical procedures, etc. Patients who fail to ask may later be surprised to learn that treatment can be denied on the basis of "pre-existing conditions" or some other pretext. An ounce of prevention is surely worth a pound of cure.

Besides procedures, the informed medical consumer also knows about the wide variety of medical specialists and other health professionals who serve a community. Remember, medical doctors have historically trained in very narrow specialties and rarely understand or appreciate treatment options outside their realms. The treatment of plantar fascitis, better known as heel spur syndrome, is a classic example. The connective tissues in the soles of the feet can get calcium deposits, or "spurs," when they are strained. While an orthopedic surgeon is trained to remove the spurs surgically, a podiatrist is able to make shoe inserts, called orthotics, which relieve the stress on the affected tissue bands. Any athlete who has suffered this problem will tell you that the medical option of surgery should be avoided in favor of the podiatrist's care. The same goes for a variety of other health services described later.

Finally, the informed medical consumer knows his rights. To illustrate the point, let's consider the issue of privacy. By now, almost all of us know someone who has contracted AIDS. Besides the mental and physical suffering, AIDS patients have a genuine fear of losing their livelihood and critical health benefits. They know that once their condition becomes public knowledge, employers, insurers, and medical facilities will try to distance themselves for one obvious reason: costs. Even though you may never get AIDS, the health care establishment still gathers and distributes potentially damaging information about you. Have you ever checked through your medical records? Others probably did. Have you ever read the release forms you signed at the clinic or before a physical exam? All are designed to protect the health care professionals or facilities. They are also made available to insurance companies and anyone else who may have a financial or legal interest.

The arrival of the information age will hasten this process. Genetic scientists are now able to identify peoples' predispositions for certain diseases with relatively simple laboratory tests of blood or other body tissues. Medical records of the future will not only reflect past illnesses, but also future prognoses, like Alzheimers, based on genetic and hereditary analysis. Once recorded in a digital format, your body chemistry and genetic data will be available on the internet, like a credit report, to a variety of users. Employers, insurance companies, and others would like to use this information as a "screening" device. Would you pick co-workers on the basis of hormone or cholesterol levels? At some point in the future, public concern will probably force the government to establish confidentiality rules. In the meantime, you need to be aware that your medical records are not simply there for your health!

Lifestyle Choices

A 50-year-old American looks like a kid when compared to a Russian of the same age. That's what visitors returning from the former Soviet Union report. Why? Public health experts would quickly point out that the two groups have experienced vastly different life styles. A combination of factors such as smoking, alcohol consumption, diet, exercise, and environmental pollution determine a person's physical state. Most Americans do pay attention to their health and also enjoy a much cleaner natural environment. Of course, health-conscious people also fall victim to disease. Hereditary factors play a role, and even doctors cannot explain the origins of brain cancer or certain other ailments. The point is, you do have control over your health! Think of it as wearing a seat belt; refusing to buckle-up won't kill you, but using belts dramatically increases survival rates of all accident victims.

A good life style consists of several basic components, such as nutrition, exercise, adequate rest, avoidance of environmental pollutants, and reduction of extreme stress. No surprises, right? Moreover, the basic ideas have been around a long time. Al Neuharth, founder of *USA Today*, reminisced about his visit with Dr. Alton Ochsner, the late health guru who created a world renowned medical center in New Orleans. Ochsner, who lived to be 85, offered this down-to-earth advice long ago:

> *Don't Smoke
> * Exercise Daily
> *Eat intellegently, but heartily
> *Drink, but in moderation
> *Keep your mind as busy as your body

Wellness: It Pays to be Healthy in the Future

There's good news and bad news on the health front. The good news is that more Americans are becoming health conscious. Researchers have found that improved diet, particularly fat reduction, has dramatically reduced death rates from stroke and heart disease in the past two decades. The same can be said about declining tobacco consumption and reduced cancer rates. At the same time, more people are exercising and doing other things to stay well. The bad news also comes from government statistics: Far too many folks, like my co-worker Jerry, are still overweight, out of shape, or have habits which make them prime candidates for early death or disability. We still have a long way to go.

Healthy people have always enjoyed more active, fulfilling lives. In the future, health-related life styles will also be linked to people's finances. In a nutshell, the managed health providers, described in the previous chapter, will either reward or punish us for our behavior. The reason is cost control. Employers, insurance companies and health care facilities are all looking for ways to cut expenses. Until recently, providers were passive and treated illnesses as they occurred. Now, they're taking the "upstream" approach to cost control, using aggressive steps to prevent illness and keeping people out of the medical system in the first place. You may have noticed periodic "health tips" from your insurance company or hospital in the mail box. In addition, imaginative employers give workers complimentary memberships to the local YMCA, health club, or even corporate fitness center. This may seem like a fringe benefit to you, but it's also the bosses' way of keeping doctor bills down. They only *pose* as philanthropists!

The most aggressive organizations are starting to use hard financial incentives. Business researchers found that many health insurance claims were due to preventable illnesses, and that employees with high coronary "risk factors," like smoking and high blood pressure, filed far more claims than those with no risks. Now, people who smoke or flunk their cholesterol tests can expect to pay a premium for health insurance coverage. Those who follow wellness guidelines can expect a rebate. Once you realize that health is not a "free" commodity, you'll understand why it's so important to become your own doctor.

My doctor agrees and recommends learning self-diagnosis, while keeping track of personal health-related information. Don't toss out those leaflets from the Heart Association or Cancer Society. They contain important information on how to nip serious diseases in the bud. You'll also discover how different physical conditions are interrelated. My friend Gene recently learned that when the neck size of a man's shirt exceeds 17, he is likely to be a snorer and suffer from sleep apnea. Why? It seems that excess neck tissues of overweight people collapse during sleep and block the breathing passages. This, in turn, causes snoring or, worse yet, sleep apnea, in which the sleeper stops breathing and continuously wakes up, robbing him or her of a good night's rest. In this case, weight management might be the key to solving a number of health problems. You should also monitor your health over time. Whenever you get a physical exam, ask the nurse for a copy of the lab reports for your personal records. They might chuckle, but you'll gain greater control of your health over time.

Shape Up or Else?

While all of this makes good business sense, people with less than perfect bodies or life styles have a right to be nervous. Americans fiercely protect their rights to personal liberty and privacy. Tobacco is a great example. For many decades, cigarettes were a common part of the American landscape. Can you imagine a Western setting without a Marlboro man? Eventually, mountains of medical evidence caused us to change our behavior and stigmatize those who couldn't break the habit. Whether in office buildings, airlines or restaurants, fewer and fewer public facilities permit smoking. Yet, there soon may be a backlash; smokers resent various restrictions throttling their right to enjoy a legal product associated with the nation's history from precolonial times.

The smokers' case makes more sense if we consider other products and habits which have a negative health effect. Can you imagine corporations of the future subjecting their employees to continuous blood and urine tests, weigh-ins, treadmill races, and the like? Or some type of a health-nazi patrol, searching briefcases and purses for twinkies, cigarettes, pep pills, or other contraband? Ultimately, there will have to be a balance between the individual's right to a self-determined life style and society's refusal to subsidize self-destructive behavior. Remember, too, that not all health problems are self-inflicted. Firm laws are needed to keep organizations from arbitrarily "selecting out" potential health risks which are not behavior related. Considering current trends, this is likely to replace race and gender as the "Equal Opportunity/Affirmative Action" issue of the next century.

Aging and Health

There is still no single, clear explanation for biological aging. However, scientists have identified a number of interrelated factors. One is genetic and focuses on hereditary factors. Laboratory studies on worms and fruit flies have demonstrated than "longevity" and "death" genes exist and can be manipulated to slow or accelerate the aging process in these lower animals. As of yet, no human "longevity" gene has been found, but don't be surprised to read about it some day. Other theories focus on human cells and how the genetic material wears down, losing its capacity to reproduce correctly over time. The wrinkled or discolored skin of elderly individuals is an example of this. The extreme form is cancer, in which radiation, chemical interference, or other irritants have caused cells to mutate and grow out of control.

Can aging be delayed? Environmental factors, exercis, and nutrition are said to play a role in the physical aging process. Regular exercise helps keep cells oxygenated, while proper nutrition helps repair and nourish cells. Dr. Roy Walford, a UCLA gerontologist, discovered that undernourished mice lived longer and had fewer diseases than fellow rodents who dined on more generous portions. Walford, who is testing the theory by starving himself, believes that excessive nutrition creates more free radicals and by-products, which damage and age cells. It seems that calorie restrictions take a load off cells and organs alike. Many nutritionists believe that human beings subsisted on very austere diets for most of our evolutionary history, and that our digestive and metabolic systems sometimes get overpowered by the highly concentrated, refined foods designed to satisfy modern taste cravings.

We know that average life spans have been almost doubled since colonial times. The consensus among scientists is that people of the next century should be able to celebrate birthdays well into the 120s. Unfortunately, the "health span" has not kept pace with the life span; so much progress has been made in extending life, but far too little in keeping people active and healthy during those years. We are still far from curing, preventing, or postponing most major diseases associated with aging. Medical ethicists say that by extending the life span, society is also doomed to experience more suffering from disease and disability. For example, Alzheimer's Disease is nothing new; previous generations usually did not live long enough to experience the full measure of this devastating affliction. Now almost everyone seems to have an elderly relative whose mind no longer functions, while nursing homes are racing to construct special units for Alzheimer's patients. That's a sobering thought when we consider the economic prospects and demographic imperatives of a large elderly population in the next century. If nothing else, current medical research needs to make age-related diseases and disabilities top priorities.

Be Your Own Doctor: Investing in Lifetime Health

According to the standard guidebooks, people of all ages should follow the same basic wellness guidelines. That means physical and mental activity, eating right, and maintaining a positive set of values and attitudes. Nothing could be worse than segregating older people from the mainstream of life and treating them as useless weaklings. That tends to become a self-fulfilling prophecy.

Like any other investment, lifetime wellness has its costs. One is knowledge, and the other is self-discipline. The medical industry of the future is likely to shower us with health wisdom, but who has the strength of character to do all the right things? First, there is food. Regardless of what the health gurus say, reduced-calorie foods rarely taste good. What they don't tell you is that fat carries the flavor. Nevertheless, it makes sense to follow the Surgeon General's guidelines and concentrate on complex carbohydrates and unprocessed fruits and vegetables with minimal meat and animal fats. Dairy products, which provide calcium for the body, should be of the low-fat variety.

The trick is to get a full measure of nutrition without overloading the body with excess calories. It's harder than you think, because the food industry makes its profits by processing foods. Typically, processing removes nutrients, while adding calories, additives, and a higher shelf price. In the case of breakfast cereal, the manufacturer takes perfectly good wheat, oats, or other grains and grinds, cooks, and bakes them into little flakes, and then adds sugar, artificial flavor, color, and preservatives. Despite some added vitamins, the nutritional value of the final product has been substantially reduced through processing and storage. Have you read any good food labels lately?

Forecasts about the food industry suggest that the trend toward more frozen and precooked "convenience foods" is far from complete. Cooking from "scratch" requires so much time and effort that many future kitchens will essentially be limited to storage bins for frozen or irradiated meals and microwave ovens to heat them. Even now, the frozen food section is your grocer's most profitable operation. Schools, factories, hospitals, and other organizations which serve meals have already begun to close the traditional cafeteria kitchens in favor of prepared, manufactured foods. It also helps them reduce labor costs. Information age automation and mass production are dramatically changing the once labor-intensive food industry.

Since the profits from prepared "quick" foods are so high, manufacturers are pushing them with relentless advertising. One example is the canned "total nutrition" drinks aimed primarily at senior citizens. In reality, they're little more than a milk shake with a vitamin pill. Doctors and nutritionists note that these drinks are appropriate for sick people with digestion problems, but are a poor substitute for the fiber-rich fresh foods our bodies really need.

Meanwhile, the restaurant business, particularly the fast food segment, is predicted to flourish in the next century. Their menus are legendary for cholesterol saturation. It's a typical situation where industrial processes and economic incentives don't meet human needs. You wonder if the Wendy's hamburger chain "lightened" its menu after Dave Thomas, the founder, suffered a massive heart attack. You will recall that advertisements featured the chunky "Burger Baron" as his own best customer. On his recovery, Thomas praised the quick response of the local emergency medical team, but had little to say about the causes of heart failure. Since the entire food industry is unlikely to change course, it becomes your responsibility to look after personal and family nutritional needs. That means staying informed and taking the trouble to select and prepare whole-some, unprocessed foods. Think of it as an investment in your health. Sure, it takes more effort to cut up fresh vegetables or search out a lean cut of meat, but the long-term results are truly worth it.

What about exercise? According to the nation's leading health experts, it should be at the top of your daily "to do" list. Here, again, good advice can be found at your local YMCA, hospital wellness center, and the like. Exercise, like nutrition, takes an investment in will power, time, and effort to do the right thing. Fitness experts say that exercise should be a life-long activity and not restricted to any age group. This means having plenty of physical activity in childhood and continuing through a lifetime. Just as other interests change, you may progress from hop scotch and tennis to speed walking and yoga over the years. What counts is that you never neglect this part of your life. There is a powerful temptation to let other activities like work, family obligations, or shopping interfere. Saying that you just don't have the time and will get to it later is the worst thing you can do. Folks who think they're too busy or important to exercise should know that business researchers report a much higher level of fitness activities among top executives than their underlings. Don't you want to be more like the boss?

There's a science to making physical activity fun and productive. Be sure you have a plan or routine which includes daily or alternate day activities. That makes it important and keeps it high on your list of priorities. More serious folks tend to use elaborate systems for exercising various parts of their bodies, like swimming and jogging on alternate days of the week. Less motivated people should look for fun: Many sports offer camaraderie and friendly competition when done in the company of others. Aerobic exercise classes are said to be a great way to meet people and socialize while sweating off the pounds!

If you exercise regularly, you already know the benefits. It's much more than abstract cardiovascular fitness or muscle tone. These activities help you to look and feel better, both of which are substantial assets in your personal and professional lives at any age. Physical strength and endurance help to make all tasks easier. Finally, let's not forget the mental benefits of regular exercise. Participants will tell you that they experience a deep sense of relaxation or anxiety release after a workout. That's because nature's own tranquilizer, endorphins, are released while physical activity occurs. Increased oxygenation of the brain also triggers creative thinking among many people while they run, walk, or paddle a canoe. A combination of these physical and mental benefits are the cornerstone of a long and active life.

This brings us to the subject of mental health. Mental and emotional problems can occur at any stage of life and deserve proper attention. For a long time, older people were automatically stereotyped as senile or feeble-minded. Current research suggests that regular exercise of the mind, like the body, keeps it from deteriorating. Other factors also play a role. For instance, when doctors examined a group of feeble-minded elders at a nursing home, they discovered that nutritional deficiencies were largely to blame for the patients' poor mental states. Mild exercise, which improves blood circulation to the brain, was also effective. It proves again how various aspects of our life style are interrelated.

Jane, who does my hair, told me how much her dad was looking forward to his retirement; he'd had it with rush-hour traffic, callous supervisors, and the whole rat race at the plant. When I recently asked Jane how her dad was doing, she almost cried. It seemed that he was now sitting at home, watching daytime TV, and feeling utterly useless and angry at the world. If you asked his wife, she'd say he had become a sort of nuisance and parasite in his own home. Why?

Jane's dad and countless others prove that depression is the single greatest mental affliction among older adults. Middle-aged and elderly white men are particularly vulnerable. Typically, they're not prepared for life without the daily job routine. It's particularly easy to lose your sense of purpose and self-esteem when forced early retirement or disabilities put you on the sidelines and ruin those "golden years" you'd dreamed about. Fortunately, depression is treatable with counseling, medication, and behavioral therapy. The fact that many elders now survive and must live with disabilities has created a suicide boom. Did you know that there are far more suicides than homicides in our country? Elders' suicides are generally covered up and don't make the news. Women, who also suffer their share of depression, do so earlier in life and are culturally conditioned to be more accepting of life's disappointments. We can expect this problem to become more serious with larger numbers of retirees in future decades. Research in the prevention and treatment of mental illness is a great investment in the general health and well-being of aging Baby Boomers in the next century.

The last, and commonly overlooked, component of good health is adequate rest. Are you aware that our ancestors averaged about 10 hours of sleep a night? Historians who have traced the nation's health habits noted that the invention of electric light made it possible to stay up much later. As a result, people nowadays average only seven hours of night sleep. Doctors say that the need for sleep varies from person to person, but that most folks probably do not get adequate rest. An afternoon nap may compensate for a short night and is part of the unpublicized daily routine of many important people including U.S. presidents. Unfortunately, most of us still consider this a sign of laziness and self-indulgence. The restorative powers of sleep will be stressed in the next century. Have you noticed how "sleep clinics" have started popping up in your community?

Fountains of Youth at the Mall?

Business forecasters agree that anti-aging products and services will experience explosive growth in the next decades. We're talking about pills, lotions, and even machinery which claims to keep us slim, help us sleep better, regrow hair, and make us more exciting romantic partners. Few of these preparations and devices are prescribed by the doctor; most are offered through mail-order catalogs, health food stores, and herbal boutiques. Furthermore, many of these products are surrounded by controversy and deserve a closer look.

The trend began years ago when scientists discovered that the human body needed minute quantities of certain minerals and vitamins to function effectively. Deficiencies could result in disease. Sufficient amounts are normally found in a well-balanced diet. Still, fear of shortages led to the development of vitamin pills and fortified foods. Since then, many nutritional experts have raised the claim that extra large doses of various vitamins and minerals could make the body perform far beyond expectations.

Do you take mega-doses of Vitamin C for a cold? Well, these nutrients are said to have medicinal value to boot, and the health food industry has started calling them Nutriceuticals. Some healing claims are supported by clinical studies, but others are very questionable and rely on testimonials of "cured" individuals. Unfortunately, real scientific proof remains elusive, since the U. S . Food and Drug Administration rarely investigates medical claims for food components. People who sell vitamins, minerals, and other food supplements prefer to keep the FDA out of it; they contend that government bureaucrats and the medical profession are out to maintain a monopoly on the healing arts and conspire to block public access to various safe, "natural " remedies which are not under their control.

Herbal remedies, hormonal preparations, and glandular extracts are even more controversial. While some doctors support their use, they are typically marketed outside the medical mainstream. In all fairness, it must be said that many of today's standard pharmaceuticals were indeed derived from medicinal herbs used in traditional folk medicine. On the other hand, health claims for some products are totally outrageous. Herbs, supposedly offering a cure for everything from dandruff to cancer, can be found in these catalogs and sales brochures. Believe it or not, one mail-order house sells a line of colon care products inspired by Edgar Cayce, a psychic who communicated with spirits in the 1930s. A panel of medical experts who tested products for *Consumer Reports* warned that some preparations, such as DSMO and animal gland extracts, pose a real danger to consumers. Exotic herbs are often marketed as ancient healing and rejuvenating secrets of Tibetans and other folk healers from obscure corners of the world. Never mind that those people generally have much lower health standards than the Americans who buy the stuff!

We should neither endorse nor demonize this whole range of over-the-counter health supplies. Again, education is your best resource. When seeking guidance, use the same principle we recommended for investing: Consider the qualifications of health "advisors" and whether they stand to gain from the sale of a product. Beware of items sold as "secrets" or "miracle cures;" if it sounds too good to be true, it usually is. Just because something is natural, doesn't mean it's good for you. Finally, be aware that many people who had lucrative careers as health and nutrition gurus did not fare well themselves. Nutritionists Adele Davis and Euell Gibbon, both of whom profited by making the rest of us feel inadequate, did not benefit from their own longevity advice and died relatively young.

Let's not forget about medical devices, a related growth sector of the future. Here, the line between fraud and science is particularly narrow. One emerging product line is straight out of the information age. These are computerized machines designed to manipulate brain waves or specific parts of the brain through sounds, lights, or electrical impulses applied to the scalp.

Currently, there are already "relaxation" devices which operate on these principles. Other machines are designed to deliver anti-aging therapies. Hyperbaric chambers, particularly, will soon gain widespread popularity. These are glass and metal tanks in which people are subjected to pure oxygen at high pressures. The treatment is painless, and doctors have found that it helps heal wounds and may even restore some brain functions of stroke victims. However, it is about to be marketed as an anti-aging device, capable of revitalizing body cells when used regularly. Look for many more of these devices to appear in the next century.

Is the Doctor Always Right?

Whenever exercise makes me thirsty, I am reminded of my basic military training experience many years ago. You, too, may recall that soldiers were required to take along salt tablets and water whenever they performed strenuous exercise in hot weather. According to medical authorities, salt was necessary to help the body retain water. Current medical wisdom says that the body efficiently manages its own salt level, and that consuming additional salt is more likely to be harmful!

This is only one example of how knowledge in the field continues to evolve. Medicine is an inexact science, where new findings continually invalidate the conventional wisdom of the moment. Even doctors know that the information is confusing and contradictory at times. We've heard so much about the harmful effects of smoking. Now, scientific studies tell that smokers are less likely to suffer from Alzheimer's disease in old age. But before you light up, remember that those same medical authorities say that the potential heart disease and cancer risks of smoking far outweigh the Alzheimer's threat in old age.

It seems that we read about some dramatic new discovery every week. For years, people blamed stomach ulcers on stress and worry. Now, scientists say that bacteria are the culprit. Other harmful microorganisms are suspected of helping form the arterial plaque which, by clogging arteries, causes strokes and heart attacks. There's a positive side as well. Did you know that widespread use of the food preservative BHA is credited with a reduction in stomach cancer in recent decades? You still wonder what dangers will be discovered next and whether some of today's health advice will turn into health warnings down the road.

The answer, of course, is that the savvy health care consumer takes his medical advice with a grain of salt. You should remember that the field of medicine, despite its infallible scientific image, is also governed by fads and fashions. Doctors want to be in touch with the latest in terms of drug therapies, diagnostic gear, etc. You would be amazed how many treatments once accorded scientific validity, like stomach freezing for ulcers, have been abandoned as ineffective or even dangerous. Meanwhile, other treatments once discredited are coming back. Leeching, for example, a common therapy in colonial days, has been validated by recent scientific insights!

Does this mean that we should ignore our doctor's advice? Definitely not. There are occasional news reports about terminal cancer patients who head to Mexico for cures based on peach pits or some other substance prohibited by the FDA. They may be the same celebrities who jetted to Romania for rejuvenating fetal sheep cell injections. The fact that American medical science is less than perfect has been used by numbers of self-proclaimed wonder doctors to discredit the entire health care establishment, while making extravagant claims for their personal "secret cures." They want you to believe that the medical establishment is conspiring to maintain its lucrative power position while keeping inexpensive and effective medicine out of the hands of ordinary people like yourself. So remember the advice from Chapter 4 on investing: If it sounds too good to be true, it probably is. Common sense should tell you where the truth lies.

The Dawn of Alternative Medicine

The high cost and general dissatisfaction with the nation's health care, as described in the previous chapter, has raised interest in various exotic treatments outside the realm of America's medical establishment. Some of these therapies are homegrown, like chiropractic and homeopathic medicine. Other alternative medicine reflects the global connection, such as the Chinese tradition of acupuncture. Asians, incidentally, are America's fastest growing ethnic minority. Besides restaurants, they maintain medical traditions from their homelands. You probably already know an adventurous person who got relief by having those pins stuck into various parts of his body. As the nation becomes more globally conscious and ethnically diverse, alternative medicine will grow in importance.

American medicine is based upon a European tradition of scientific inquiry. It is highly mechanistic and empirical and rejects anything which cannot be explained in terms of current scientific knowledge. Asian and other non-western medicine relies upon long centuries of experience. Take the case of Chinese acupuncture. It works, but neither American nor European doctors can explain it in terms of their knowledge. Other Eastern traditions, like those of India, focus on the patient's mind as the principal agent of healing. Here, the patient doesn't worry about symptoms, like blood chemistry; rather, the patient learns to achieve a state of enhanced consciousness, where "inner" forces are brought to bear on the disease. Western doctors are skeptical, but there is mounting evidence that a positive mental state does indeed strengthen the immune system and help fight cancer and related illnesses.

Alternative medicine, as described here, will play a greater role in the next century. The medical establishment is grudgingly accepting the evidence, even though traditional, test-tube science cannot be applied. In addition, these healing arts use little technology and are therefore quite cost effective. Ultimately, techniques like meditation, hypnosis, and acuputure will increase the number of medical options, particularly when used in conjunction with conventional therapies.

Have a Nice Death

What experience is only shared with those who are close to us? You guessed it: The loss of a loved one. Just last year, Pat, a secretary in the adjoining office, was diagnosed with pancreatic cancer and died less than six months later. Pat's decline was all too evident whenever we visited her in the hospital. The eerie half-lights in darkened rooms, the clicking and gurgling of life-support systems, and even the antiseptic smell of those hospital corridors always comes back to me whenever I reminisce about my friend's final days. Have you watched the decline and death of a loved one and then wondered, like me, how your end will come?

Will death be different in the next century? Despite advances in longevity, death will continue to be the inevitable conclusion to all human existence. Nevertheless, current developments in medical science will lead to a new set of values and attitudes that involve conscious choices for people facing their demise.

Technological advances may benefit humanity, but they can also create ethical quandaries. Life-sustaining medical technologies are a case in point. Years ago even minor illnesses among old folks quickly advanced to life-threatening, fatal stages. You could say that nature took its course. Current medical practice usually makes short work of minor illness and can sustain life for extended periods using intensive care technology. This raises two issues: should we maintain life when an aged patient has little chance of recovery? And can we afford the enormous costs of providing such intense, aggressive care to large numbers of terminal patients? The traditional culture of medicine required physicians to maintain life at all costs; now, the paradoxical benefit of life-sustaining technology is forcing society to reconsider this maximalist proposition.

When asked about the issue, most older people will tell you that they don't fear death very much; they fear long-term disability, the pain and helplessness of terminal illness. The best thing, it seems, would be to live a long and active life and then accept death without a long period of suffering, the byproduct of advanced medical science. Although the subject is still taboo, people in the next century can expect to have more choices in selecting the time and circumstances of their final moments.

The Hospice movement, originated in Great Britain, was a step in that direction. Hospice is a treatment concept limited to providing comfort and pain relief for terminally ill patients. Physicians, trained to regard a patient's death as professional failure, originally frowned on allowing nature to take its course. Today, though, the hospice has become a part of the medical mainstream, and doctors are learning to accept death as a natural part of life.

The next step was the introduction of "living wills." Basically, it's a statement from a patient spelling out his or her wish not to prolong death by futile medical procedures. Normally, these "advance directives" are executed when a person has full control of his faculties and take effect when the patient is no longer conscious or capable of communicating. The idea is to let people make a rational choice about their fate, rather than letting an impersonal doctor or hysterical relatives take control. Medical professionals must determine whether the patient's case is really hopeless and then act accordingly. While it may be both brave and prudent to decline resuscitation when facing imminent death, cynics counter that this is still another way for the health care industry to save money on elderly patients. To be sure, a number of states have enacted "Natural Death Laws," and hospital patients are handed Advanced Directive forms at the admission station.

Euthanasia is the final step along this path. Unlike the living will, it goes beyond refusal of treatment and actually allows a mortally ill patient to choose death. Some call it "death with dignity," but others call it "suicide under medical supervision." To be sure, depressed, terminally sick people have taken their own lives to escape continued pain and suffering. The motives vary. Some folks are simply fed up with life's decline; others are altruistic, deciding to leave their accumulated assets to children or charity rather than having them sucked up by a monstrous final medical bill. One Florida couple did just that. Nearing death, they decided to commit suicide and leave their wealth to a church charity rather than use it for futile care of their deteriorating bodies.

While individual suicide no longer carries the stigma it once did, the physician's role in assisting people is quite controversial. From the viewpoint of the terminal patient, a doctor is needed to make sure that the procedure is painless and doesn't get botched. You have no idea how many suicide attempts fail, leaving the individual in much worse circumstances than before. It certainly runs counter to the traditional ethical guidelines of the medical profession! Nevertheless, physicians in some European countries, notably the Netherlands, have helped long-suffering, terminal patients end their ordeal with overdoses of pain-killing drugs. Despite opposition from some religious authorities, courts have supported the practice when it is carried out under sanctioned guidelines. Few American doctors have dared to do this openly, but confidential surveys of intensive care personnel revealed that some consider it an act of mercy to guide a dying patient to the final exit.

Active, involuntary euthanasia, where a physician causes death without the patient's knowledge or consent, is unlikely to gain moral acceptance in the foreseeable future. Even if well intentioned, it smacks of murder and runs counter to our ethical values. Assisted suicide, on the other hand, will become commonplace in the next century. Think of it as the ultimate health care choice. That's because the accomplishments of medical technology have created the much more gruesome alternative of being maintained artificially in a half-life state. As the issue is debated in legislatures and courts, look for the hot issue of medical costs to be considered; granting the "right to die" may not only be humane, but also cost effective in a society with numerous elderly people. Medical ethicists of the 21st century are likely to support the principle that an individual's autonomy should be maintained until the final moment.

Chapter 7

YOUR HOME OR YOUR PIGGY BANK?
Housing in the 21st Century

Pick up the real estate section of the Sunday paper, and you'll read gushy descriptions of self-contained castles built by Baby Boomers in remote forests and on mountain tops. The mood of the 90s was one of escaping from urban problems and settling in pristine rural settings, far from the maddening crowd. Trading up to larger, more luxurious homes was another phenomenon of this generation as it reached mid-life. Luxury, by the way, was also a necessity, since home ownership represented the most solid investment for the future.

Look for a different set of real estate stories in the next century. Most likely, they'll feature news about retirement communities, population migration, and economic hardships caused by the collapse of suburban real estate markets. Other stories will feature prefab homes and other technological innovations in building design and construction, as the housing industry responds to an age of greater frugality. Yes, the demographic, technological, and economic developments of the next century are certain to shatter many current ideas about housing and home ownership.

The Baby Boom as Building Boom

Housing experts have described the home-building fever of the Baby Boom years as the greatest construction period since the pyramids. It began in the late 40s, when the Boomers' parents began to nest, and it hardly abated until the last Boomers finally established their own homes during the late eighties. The same period, you will recall, was also marked by explosive economic growth and optimism. Furthermore, generous government policies, like those which pumped up Social Security, also subsidized middle-class home buyers in various ways.

A number of other factors pushed the trend along. Recall that the Boomers' parents were the ones who bought the cars, built the highways, and moved from urban centers into suburbs. Matured war bonds, working wives, and rising wages suddenly gave large numbers of working families the means to achieve the American Dream: a home of their own and a place to park that new Nash or Studebaker. Although prosperous as never before, the new middle class received government housing subsidies as a bonus! Uncle Sam guaranteed home loans through the Veterans Administration and later through the Federal Housing Administration as well. Everyone, including the wealthy home buyer, was further subsidized by mortgage interest tax deductions. Low-income and public housing were largely ignored; the economic and political clout of the moment rested with single-family home builders and buyers outside the city limits.   Sadly, suburbanization and the departure of the productive middle class were also decisive factors in the decay of America's inner cities.

Ask members of the older generation about the wisest financial decision they ever made and almost all will tell you that it was real estate. I'm sure you've heard stories similar to that of Uncle George and Aunt Grace who worked hard in the years following World War II to save for the down payment on their new place in the country. In 1952 it was a long drive to their jobs in the city, and the kids had no real neighborhood school. But the country life was pleasant and peaceful, as they tended their garden and hiked in the surrounding forest on the weekends. Soon, however, they were joined by other houses, followed by stores, churches, and eateries. The roads were four-lane in the 60s, and then came apartment complexes and office buildings. When George and Grace left for Florida in the late 80s, their neighborhood had been transformed from a muddy dirt road in the country to an expanse of concrete and glass with very few green spaces left. In a way, the city had followed them. There's nostalgia in their voices when they show you faded photos of their house, which has disappeared to make place for a McDonald's parking lot. On the other hand, the ultimate return on their initial investment was incredible. Even figuring for inflation, the 50-fold increase in value on their land was sufficient for a very comfortable Florida retirement.

Yes, the advantages of home ownership were great and magnified still further by the booming real estate market. The demand was incredible. It seemed that no matter what you bought, it could be resold to an eager buyer at a much higher price after only a short time. Professional real estate people earned fortunes, while even ordinary home buyers could speculate successfully in a market which knew only how to go up. In earlier times, people had acquired a home to last them a lifetime. But by the 70s and 80s, folks leapfrogged to successively bigger homes, as their credit limits permitted. After all, each change in housing status quickly translated into a higher personal net worth, or so it seemed. Houses, in other words, were more than just a home; they had become a family's principal financial investment and ticket to a prosperous future. Europeans, by the way, were puzzled and amused by Americans who subsisted on a steady diet of macaroni and cheese so that they could afford to pay for those lavish suburban palaces.

All Bubbles Must Burst

Even cracker box houses, bought for a song in the 1940s and 1950s, fetched stunning prices when resold to desperate young families a few decades later. Many in the Boomers' parent generation proved that point and reaped a true windfall. However, the real estate boom came to a screeching halt for most of the country in the late 1980s. Just like the fall of the Berlin Wall, no one had anticipated such a development; yet, in retrospect, the underlying reasons were clear. Decisive demographic and economic forces, unleashed much earlier, were finally catching up. For one thing, the supply of housing had grown faster than the Baby Boomers' needs, which were rapidly becoming saturated. Other factors included an abbreviation of this generation's housing requirements because of fewer children and a larger proportion of unmarried adults. Financial factors, such as economic insecurity and dramatically higher interest rates, also slowed down the real estate merry-go-round. Most folks took a deep breath and lived on, particularly if their mortgage debts were adequately covered by salary or other income. Some, however, experienced serious losses, especially if they had speculated or were forced to sell at a loss when making a job transfer to another town. Many urban elderly people are scratching their heads right now. It seems that their neighborhoods have decayed over the past several decades, and nobody around them can get financing for a decent offer on their big, creaky, old homes.

How good an investment is your home in the next century? There's still truth in the traditional wisdom that the earth is finite and real estate prices must rise in the long run. At the same time, we should reiterate once more that the baby boom and its wide-ranging excesses represented a detour from the nation's historical development. The 50s, 60s, and 70s simply were not "normal" in terms of demographically-determined economic developments. Of all the balloons to be popped at the end of this era, housing was perhaps the single biggest one.

In the future, home ownership will be a good, but not a great, investment. There are, of course, exceptions which we will discuss later. First, buying a house or condominium is a form of forced savings, which most folks don't do enough of anyway. Even if prices fall, a homeowner will be better off than a renter at the point of sale.

Built-up equity in an owner occupied house offers a financial cushion that renters simply don't enjoy. Think of it as another savings account. In an emergency, this nest egg could be tapped in the form of a second mortgage, and everyone knows about the financial advantage of "home equity" loans. On the other hand, real estate prices are no longer guaranteed to rise automatically, and speculation becomes a dangerous game. Under normal circumstances, you should not put more of your family assets into a house than what is needed to provide a comfortable home. Some folks who had over-leveraged themselves in the late eighties actually walked out when their house value dropped below mortgage value a few years later. You may remember seeing the painful sights of new, but abandoned, subdivisions in Texas and other regions of the Southwest. The truly unfortunate home buyers were then sued for the difference by the mortgage lender!

Demographic Trends and Future Real Estate Values

As we learned in Chapter 4 on Investments, the basic strategy for finding future value is to project the evolving needs and assets of the Baby Boomers. Social scientists note that every stage in life, or family setting, ideally requires a different form of housing. One type of home, with a fenced yard and suburban setting, is ideal for rearing children. Another home, perhaps a downtown condominium, makes more sense for singles or childless professional couples. Finally, congregate housing caters to the special needs of mature or aging folks.

From this perspective, the future housing needs of Baby Boomers are quite clear. Now at middle age, they will soon conclude child-rearing years. The lucky ones are reaching top salaries. This explains the continued boom in luxurious "trophy" homes, compared to stagnation in most other real estate categories. But in the early decades of the next century, the affluent ones will begin shopping for retirement digs, and by the 2030s most of them will be living with children or in retirement communities. Ultimately, their housing will merge with old-age care in a quasi-medical setting. In other words, the future real estate market will be largely shaped by that generation's transition from mid-life to old-age.

Now, let's make the forecasts more specific. To begin with, the housing situation of today's senior citizens offers some insights into what will happen on a larger scale in the next century. For instance, intergenerational families once inhabited large homes in and around urban centers. As the younger generation left for the outskirts, older people frequently found themselves in a deteriorating house which had become too big for their needs and would ultimately have to be abandoned at a fraction of their earlier value. The simultaneous influx of poor and unemployed people, beset by crime, drugs, and other social problems, lowered housing values still further. The well-publicized urban renewal and restoration of such neighborhoods typically results in gentrification which former residents can't afford.

So you think that property values in the suburbs are immune to such precipitous price slides? Think again. Recall that the suburban subdivisions were essentially created for young, growing families, where the bread winner rose at dawn for a long commute to work. Very soon, more and more of these homes will become unsuitable for the occupants' retirement years. First, size and upkeep will probably be unmanageable for senior citizens. Then, rising utility costs, like heating in the Northeast, will eat into austere retirement incomes. Paradoxically, the relative isolation of the suburbs, their former charm, will be hardest for elder people to bear. Suburbanites relied almost exclusively on cars for commuting to work, shopping, recreation, and all other transportation needs. Considering Americans' disdain for public transportation, suburban life would have been totally impossible without the automobile. Unfortunately, that's exactly the situation many elderly people will face, as deteriorating vision and other disabilities deprive them of their "wheels." Then, there's the climate. Scraping icy windshields and shoveling snow may be fun when you're young, but certainly they lose this charm as the years go by. Every winter, it seems, you hear stories of elders who have become isolated and trapped in their own home. Unless public transportation loses its stigma and makes a comeback, most of these folks will be forced to relocate to retirement communities, group homes, or other locations which don't pose a transportation problem.

In the next century, members of Generation X can find relief from their other hardships by shopping for fine homes at bargain prices in outlying areas. That's the good news for young folks. The bad news is that their parents will not have left them very much for the down payment. In terms of inheritance, middle-class Baby Boomers profited mightily from their elders' real estate bonanza. The next generation, unfortunately, can anticipate only flat returns on parents' home investments. Worse yet, Baby Boomers, known as a generation of spendthrifts, may have to use their housing equity to finance retirement and health care during their waning years. That would leave even less for the heirs.

Although not well known yet, the mechanism is already in place. It's called "reverse mortgage" and allows elderly people to receive cash income from selling their homes while they still live in them. Typically, senior citizens work out a deal with real estate investors who give them a monthly mortgage check, while permitting them to remain in the house for the rest of their lives. Naturally, elders can't command top dollar, since the formal change of ownership cannot be predicted precisely. Nevertheless, it is a workable solution for the many senior citizens who can be described as house rich and cash poor. Like the viatical life insurance settlement described in Chapter 5, this will allow the next generation of senior citizens to finance the expenses of a longer life span with current assets, which in earlier times would have been passed on as an estate to their heirs.

21st Century Homes: Factory Direct?

Popular forecasts of future housing tend to focus on various gadgets and convenience items like stereos which start the music as you enter a room or strategically-placed surveillance cameras to monitor bratty kids. The real changes are in construction and will be far more profound. Housing experts claim that home-building techniques still lag far behind other industrial processes in America. In an age when almost everything else is mass produced, many houses are still built on a brick by brick basis. Actually, the technology for more efficient construction is not that new. During the 1930s the mail order company Sears & Roebuck shipped many frame house "kits," which were then assembled on location. Although somewhat plain and uniform in appearance, these factory homes proved themselves to be quite durable over the years. Currently, mobile homes, less affectionately known as trailers, are the fastest-growing housing category in America. Even the most elaborate "double wide" models, with fireplaces and sunken tubs, are mass produced at a factory.

The future belongs to "modular" construction. Instead of attempting to build a whole house at the factory, rooms, walls, and roof sections are prefabricated and then joined together, like

Lego toys, on a concrete foundation at the building site. As the price of wood rises, steel will become the building material of choice. Besides its stability, steel is also resistant to termites, warping, and rot. This type of home is much more solid and durable than a trailer and also can be "customized" with different panel shapes and sizes. Cost is the main advantage over traditional "stick-built" houses. First, industrial mass production techniques are much more efficient and saves on labor costs. Secondly, inclement weather, which typically halts building activity during Northern winters, is no longer a factor at the heated and air-conditioned plant. Finally, the on-site construction phase is much faster once the components are there. Early models of these prefabricated homes are starting to find buyers in the Northeast, where construction has always been more difficult and expensive. The continued spread of these houses will be nearly "invisible," since the outside appearance is indistinguishable from the rest.

Along with the modular building, you can expect to order customized prefab interiors like optional equipment for a car. This will make the home more livable for folks at different life stages. Young families will likely want floors and walls which are easy to clean, child-proof cabinet doors, and other features to make their "rug rats" safe and comfortable. Custom features for older people will receive the greatest attention.

Considering the high cost of institutional care, expect an all-out effort to redesign housing for independent living, even when the occupant is frail and partially disabled. To get a better understanding of requirements, ask someone in a wheel chair. Obviously, single-level floor plans are best, and stairways are out. Other features might include grab bars in the bathroom, "soft tubs," made of resilient materials, door levers in place of knobs, crank-operated windows, and the like. Ultimately, the demand will become so great that even standard houses will acquire some of these user-friendly features.

Care to visit someone's "dream house" in the middle of the next century? Don't look for a luminous globe on stilts or other bold shapes you've seen in science fiction flicks. Most futurists believe that people will be craving tradition and continuity with the past. In other words, expect colonial, Cape Cod, and other traditional styles on the outside. Once inside, the decor may also look familiar, but this is deceptive. To begin with, this "smart" house will be wired to a central computer which serves to control climate, lighting, security systems, and a host of other things we now do manually. That same system also connects residents to the outside world, where functions such as telephone, TV, and the internet will have been combined into a single carrier.

Although the residents crave privacy, electronic links to the outside world become increasingly important as more and more professionals "telecommute" from home offices. You may recall from Chapter 2 that the traditional home/office dichotomy is on the way out. Some of your more savvy friends are probably already conducting business from their homes and reaping the generous tax benefits. With the modular building style described earlier, folks will be able to add on bedrooms, baths, and furnished home offices as their lifestyles change and other needs arise.

The biggest surprise, no doubt, will be in terms of individualism and creativity fostered by the future home. For those who can afford it, the home will be a source of personal self-expression. Living in a robotic and dehumanized environment, people will find joy and stimulation through music, arts, sports, horticulture, and other avocations. While the environment has the potential to turn everyone into a couch potato, people will find themselves challenged to create a world of originality and personal meaning. Gourmet cookery, home wine making, orchid cultivation, and a host of other creative endeavors in the future will make us 20th century folks look like passive, television-addicted drones. You may remember that futurists of the last century predicted that mechanical transportation would turn the human race into a breed of flabby weaklings. They should have lived long enough to witness the sports and fitness craze of the 1980s and 1990s! Believe me, the next century holds similar surprises.

Finally, the home of the next century may well include a quiet place for thought, meditation, and spiritual quest. No video or other electronic devices here, please. Evidence is already mounting that many folks are becoming alienated by the artificial and manipulative aspects of information age mass culture. Not surprisingly, a number of futurists predict a revival of spirituality and religion in the next century. Whether "New Age" or traditional in orientation, it is certain that the 21st century mindset will crave depth, authenticity, and a life of the spirit which transcends the increasingly mechanical world.

Population Migrations: America on the Move

Everyone knows that Florida has been colonized by elderly New Yorkers, but the true extent of population migrations in America is far more extensive and complex than that. Furthermore, forecasters expect migration to accelerate in the next century. Let us examine who's moving where, and then consider how all of us will be affected by this population turbulence in the next century.

Actually, when you think about it, our nation's history from the time of the Mayflower has been one of a restless people moving about. Even before then, many of the Indians regularly migrated in search of more fertile land and better hunting grounds. Current and future migrations are simply a continuation of our national past. Instead of following buffalo herds, young people follow jobs across the country. Major corporations and the armed forces require management personnel to make frequent moves throughout a career. Meanwhile, there has been a general population shift from the rusty, industrial regions of the Northeast and North central states to the Sunbelt, which stretches from Florida through Texas, the Southwest, and California. Chapter 2 described how America is shedding heavy industry and the industrial work force; now the warm climate and cheaper labor, energy, and land prices are drawing people to the South and West.

Many senior citizens, who are not even looking for jobs, are also migrating to the warmer climates after a lifetime of work in the Snowbelt. Most retirees remain in place, but those who do move have a considerable impact on the economy at both ends of their journey. Who moves? Gerontologists claim that today's elderly are much more cosmopolitan and travel-wise than earlier generations. They are typically prosperous and able-bodied "young old," with a hankering to return to an earlier vacation spot, but on a permanent basis. It's like trading snow shovels, juvenile gangs, and pot holes for the sparkling clear mountain ranges of the Southwest or the romantic palm-lined beaches of Florida. Official demographic statistics prove the lure of vacation lands: America's greatest population growth happens in counties adjacent to the water, particularly the Gulf of Mexico and the Pacific coasts. The Southwest is the other population magnet, where Las Vegas, Nevada, Laredo, Texas, and Yuma, Arizona racked up the fastest municipal growth rates in the mid-nineties. Look at the U.S. map (Figure 1) to see what's been happening. Since retirees usually want to avoid big cities, many smaller towns are experiencing a renaissance. Communities adjacent to military bases, with their medical, recreational, and shopping facilities, are magnets for retired service personnel. With the military cuts after the Cold War, such bases can expect to become retiree service centers in the next century.

When it comes to destination states, Florida is still the king. However, California, Arizona, and Texas are also drawing more elderly residents. In addition, the Carolinas are also entering the picture. Dr. Charles Longino, a gerontologist who specializes in elderly migrations, observed subtle differences

Percentage Change in the U.S. Population 65+ Between 1980 and 1990, by State

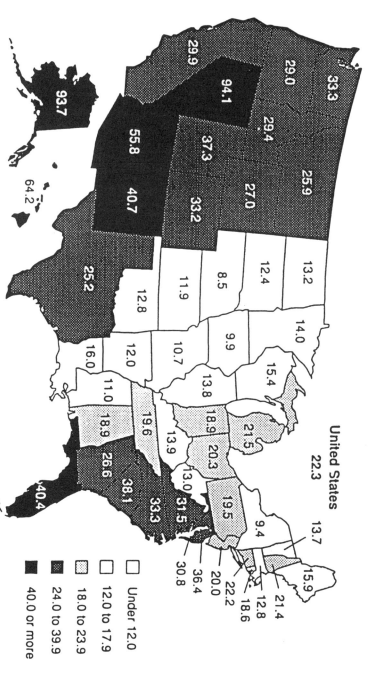

United States 22.3

Legend:
- Under 12.0
- 12.0 to 17.9
- 18.0 to 23.9
- 24.0 to 39.9
- 40.0 or more

Source: U.S. Bureau of the Census, 1980 and 1990 Census of Population and Housing

among elderly migrants. For instance, a large proportion of California's incoming elders are from Mexico and Asia, following their adult children who immigrated earlier. North Carolina draws significant numbers of native sons and daughters who had left the state for economic reasons in earlier decades. This is particularly true for Carolina born African Americans. For some reason, the Ozark mountains of Arkansas hold a special attraction for older Chicagoans.

Retirement guides, found at your book store or public library, describe and rate retirement destinations. The ratings normally include such factors as climate, housing and living costs, crime, access to recreation and culture, medical facilities and other things which make life comfortable and pleasant in a manageable setting. Fairhope, Alabama, highly rated in a recent survey, is a typical example. Fairhope is a small, picturesque town on a bluff overlooking Mobile Bay. It also has easy access to sparkling Gulf beaches, numerous golf courses, and the metropolitan centers of Mobile and Pensacola. The climate is warm, but not too hot, and the sailing is excellent. The town itself is compact, prosperous, and relatively crime free. Fairhope also has an "artsy-craftsy" reputation, since a number of well-known writers and artists makes it their home. It offers small-town, "country club" living with a little panache.

With the demise of textile manufacturing and other industries, many small and mid-sized towns in the Sunbelt have begun to recruit retirees as a form of economic development. Yes, retirees are the non-polluting "growth industry" of the future. They are the ideal citizens because they bring money, patronize local business, and support the tax base. At the same time, they are unlikely to commit crime, use the school system, or clog roadways during workday rush hours. Mississippi, Arkansas, and Alabama are the most aggressive, using national advertising campaigns and even searching for former residents who might be enticed to retire back home. Alabama's Robert Trent Jones Golf Trail was built with visitors and retirees in mind; that state also helps fund local Chambers of Commerce to attract well-off senior citizens.

As with everything else, the short and long-term consequences of these migrations vary. To begin with, the departure of prosperous retirees severely hurts the losing states and communities. They will lose economic assets and tax income from wealthier departing citizens, but must still help support the poor or disabled elderly who have no choice but to remain in place. Some states, like Pennsylvania, have given their Departments of Aging the mission of conducting ad campaigns to halt the steady exit of retirees and their assets to Florida. That, essentially, is the current situation.

If present trends continue, the tables will be turned in the next century. Many healthy and prosperous retirees of the nineties will live long enough to spend down their assets and actually become a burden to their communities of residence. "Boomerang" retirees bear this out. They are a small but growing number of migrants who moved South at one time, but then changed their minds when loneliness or disabilities drew them back to the sheltering care of their families. Most, however, will be stuck with their moves. What seems like a bonanza right now will soon come to haunt Sunbelt communities which artificially altered their demographic mix in favor of the elderly. The crushing costs of elder care, predicted for the next century, will hit them much harder. Ironically, Sunbelt voters also support the current political mantra of "smaller government." By stripping Washington of social programs and returning responsibility to local authorities, these particular states and regions will have to shoulder a much larger tax burden in the 2020s and 2030s. Don't be surprised when Congress is asked to provide "age subsidies" for those regions that once courted out-of-state elders.

In the meantime, these elders can bring unanticipated and even unwelcome changes to their adoptive communities. Many of the new arrivals are not only wealthier, but are also more aggressive and politically active than local old-timers. In

Florida, for instance, the elderly have successfully opposed taxes for school construction and other needs of young people. Elsewhere, vocal elders have blocked factory construction and other enterprises which might have benefited the larger community, but didn't suit their quality of life.

Housing Options in Later Life

Until recently, elderly people were routinely absorbed by large intergenerational families. Most likely, they had always lived in this circle of kinfolk. Adult children, typically the eldest daughter or daughter-in-law, assumed responsibility for elder care. This is still the case among Asians, Hispanics, African Americans, and other ethnic minorities who maintain a traditional family support system. Meanwhile, mainstream America has experienced social changes resulting in more nuclear families and independent elders. What does the future hold?

The "American Dream," it is said, consists of young people getting their own home. That same dream for old folks is to stay in their home. That works as long as people can manage their households. After that, the greatest number of elderly move in with adult children. Anyone who has ever experienced this, knows how traumatic this adjustment can be for all parties. Under optimal circumstances, the children can rearrange their household to give all age groups a measure of privacy and autonomy. Some houses already have a built-in "mother-in-law" apartment. Another variation of this is to place a trailer or temporary structure for the parents in the back yard. It goes by the name of ECHO, Elder Cottage Housing Opportunity, and is designed to offer a combination of privacy and closeness to both generations. Gerontologists predict that necessity will make these shared living arrangements much more common in the next century.

Affluent retirees who give up their homes have a number of options. For those who are still fit and healthy, a move to the Sunbelt may be in order. While some choose to live independently, others are moving into retirement communities specifically designed for people their age. The "grand-daddy" of these is Sun City, Arizona, which opened in 1960. Besides Arizona, clusters of these communities can be found in Florida, Texas, and California, with a smattering in other warm-climate locations. Most have either trailers or modest ranch-style houses clustered around common recreational facilities—pools, tennis courts, and even golf courses. Other amenities such as health clinics, churches, and shops round out these self-contained communities. Gates and fences usually shield residents from outside intrusion; children are admitted only as visitors. The communities pride themselves on their friendly atmosphere and non-stop hobby, culture, and sports activities. A small number of cynics, appalled by age segregation and such frantic activity in an artificial setting, scorn them as the "Land of the Living Dead."

Congregate housing is another option. These are elderly residential centers found almost everywhere, serving elders who need some supervision and care. It is possible to select one in your own town and maintain contact with family and lifelong friends. Others can be found in Sunbelt or resort settings. Local governments and churches often subsidize low-income elderly housing in this fashion. Others are pure business enterprises, offering security, specialized facilities, and an on-call nurse. The most typical arrangement involves a high-rise building, where individuals or couples occupy small apartments or rooms. The ground floor is reserved for community purposes with a dining room, clinic, library, craft shop, and other services. For well to-do-retirees, there are retirement communities which resemble country clubs or resorts, offering every imaginable civilized pleasure. Luxury hotels, which have witnessed a drop in business travelers, are also starting to recruit the upscale retired clientele as permanent residents.

Life Care or Continuing Care Communities combine apartment-like residential facilities for healthy seniors with connecting nursing homes should they become disabled or bedridden. To be admitted, a senior citizen is normally expected to be in good health and able to "purchase" his or her unit. It is assumed that the money will come from the proceeds of a home sale. In addition, there is a monthly fee to cover meals, recreational facilities, laundry, and the like. The purchase fee is nonrefundable, but will be applied to nursing home care if the need arises. Although relatively expensive, Life Care has some important advantages. First, it allows people to make conscious choices as to how and where they will spend their remaining years. Secondly, once needed, nursing care is guaranteed to be available. This also takes a burden off children and other relatives. Finally, this is an ideal arrangement for married couples who wish to remain close even if one of them becomes disabled and must have professional care.

A recent visit with Aunt Margaret, who lives at a Life Care Community called Hilltop Manor, was instructive. Margaret, a retired junior college instructor, was widowed five years ago. After Fred's death she had promised herself to continue living in their modest but comfortable suburban house. After all, they had always been actively involved in community affairs and were held in high esteem by friends and neighbors. Then came a series of minor strokes, and, even though the neighbors brought soup and cut her lawn, Margaret didn't really feel safe alone anymore. Her son Doug, she told me, had been transferred to the West Coast by his corporation.

Once Margaret decided on moving to Hilltop Manor, she faced the hard part—selling the house and dispersing its contents, a lifetime of family memories. Yes, there were tears. Fortunately, Doug was able to use his vacation to help at this stage. While much had to be discarded or given away, they were able to use a few heirlooms, photos, and treasured antiques to create a microcosm of her former home in that tiny Hilltop Manor apartment. Now, Margaret actually feels a sense of relief about the past and stoically accepts the current situation as the best of all possible worlds.

Actually, life at Hilltop Manor is not bad. Although the menus repeat themselves on a monthly basis, the food is nutritious and appetizing. Members of the staff are attentive, and there are always things to do. A bus provides regular transportation to grocery stores, malls, and entertainment events. Margaret does miss her car, but she has figured out ways to get around. On the "campus," as they like to call it, there are daily exercise classes, crafts, card tournaments, and interdenominational church services on Sundays. "Never a dull moment" is the motto of Susie, Hilltop's activity director. So what are the gripes? Some folks are grousing about the rising monthly rates and whether their retirement checks can keep pace. More than anything else, Margaret misses the company of children and young people. According to her, it's sort of like looking in a mirror with everyone you meet at Hilltop Manor. There's a dearth of older men, and those codgers who are single or widowed receive a steady supply of homemade cookies and other endearments from the Hilltop ladies. Every once in while, believe it or not, there's a wedding.

On leaving, I congratulated Aunt Margaret on her good choice in retirement living. For her, like many, it was clearly the best alternative.

As these Life Care facilities proliferate, they will also face serious problems in the next century. Specifically, some of them have underestimated the life spans of disabled residents and rising costs of caring for them. Since serving healthy residents is generally profitable, managers will try to recruit a younger clientele. Even then, many of these communities will soon face a financial squeeze or even bankruptcy from the burden of caring for large numbers of bedridden elders. That would be catastrophic for those residents who have invested life savings there.

Ultimately, residential arrangements coincide with institutional health care settings. Only a few people will have the foresight and the financial resources to select Continuing Care. Most will be shuffled to a nursing home by their adult children after some health crisis. For a while, generous Medicare and Medicaid benefits made nursing homes a fairly profitable industry. However, the anticipated austerity of 21st century health care funding will be acutely felt here. By 2020, they will likely have been merged with a quasi-public managed care organization described in the fifth chapter.

Real Estate Investment in the Third Millennium

So, do you still want to invest in real estate? Fundamentally, real estate will always be a good investment, particularly if your goal is to diversify assets. However, demographic and economic forces are about to change the rules. As with other forms of investment, it pays to understand evolving trends. Let us revisit some of these demographic, economic, and geographic determinants and see what the future holds.

To repeat, the first and most basic rule is to stay ahead of the Baby Boomer demand. Currently, that would mean looking at future residential, medical, and commercial facilities geared toward mature adults. Except in unusual circumstances, the value of single-family homes, which skyrocketed in previous decades, will stagnate and even decline. Living in your own home is great, but don't count on it as the ultimate and only investment. Remember that government policies, which formerly favored young families with subsidies and tax breaks, are shifting in favor of the older generation and its needs. You can be sure that when Baby Boomers vacate urban and suburban houses in the 2020s, the market will collapse.

Aging Baby Boomers will need housing better suited to their needs. The current generation of senior citizens is already pointing the way. Ideal housing for them will most likely consist of apartment and condominium-style accommodations. Although currently still out of favor with investors, their convenience and easy lifestyle features will be a hit with older residents in the not-too-distant future. Luxury retirement homes also offer good investment opportunities. At the same time, people should be careful about putting their money into those facilities where long-term care obligations could turn into a financial liability.

There is no question that the general population shift to the Sunbelt will continue. Urban centers of the North, once the powerhouse of the nation, will continue to lose influence and population with the decline of smokestack industries. Much the same can be said about the Midwest. Meanwhile, population will continue heading West and South, particularly toward the coastal regions. Environmental scientists contend that water shortages will eventually halt growth in the Southwest, but that is a problem for the latter part of the 21st century. Large numbers of retirees will swell this migration for the next decades, followed, of course, by younger people with careers in the "aging industry."

Investors realize that "vacation land" serves as a favorite retirement destination, full of happy memories from earlier days. Again, Florida is the numero uno, but its real estate markets may already be out of reach for many investors. Those retirees who like warm winters but are not ready or willing to make a final move will migrate seasonally. Right after Christmas, flocks of northern "snowbirds" pack up Lincoln Towncars and head south for the rest of the winter. The arrival of the snowbirds has an enormous economic impact on tourist regions which once literally died during the winter. Now condos and hotel rooms reward investors with much higher occupancy rates. Snowbirds, by the way, are not big spenders, but they're orderly and don't trash resorts like the collegiate Spring Break crowd which follows them. Since South Florida has become so saturated, the "pan-handle" and neighboring areas like the Alabama Gulf Coast are benefiting from the seasonal influx. Investors should consider resort property which is reasonable, off the beaten track, and has occupancy potential for all seasons.

Once snowbirds nest, they faithfully come back every year and even establish colonies from their home communities! For those without ties back home, these resorts are likely to become a final residence as well.

Conclusion

NOW THAT YOU KNOW:
Facing the Future with Courage and Confidence

While driving, do you ever listen to talk radio? It's my way of taking America's pulse. While much of what you hear is trivial and contrived, certain recurring themes accurately reflect the concerns of ordinary people. Folks clearly like to vent frustration, anger, and bewilderment about the changes that are happening around them. True or not, talk show callers claim that they grew up in friendly neighborhoods where no one had to lock the door at night. Nowadays, they'll tell you, crime is all around them. Why? People have lost the work ethic; everyone wants something for nothing or will steal to get it. The older generation is particularly upset about young people, spoiled in permissive schools and disrespectful of moral values. Then, there's a vague fear of not being able to make ends meet as the deteriorating financial health of Social Security and Medicare creeps into the news. Arrogant elites in Washington and Hollywood have corrupted the America they cherish. Talk show callers like to blame individuals or institutions for their problems, but you know that underlying forces of change are at work. You'd think America is going to hell in a hand basket; or is it?

Yes, the 21st century world definitely will be different, presenting mainstream Americans with bewildering and unexpected challenges and opportunities. In fact, many, if not most, future developments are inevitable. We saw in previous chapters how demographic, technological, and economic forces are forging our new world. It will be a more mature world, dominated by the needs and concerns of older people. It will also be a world where traditional concepts of work and careers dissolve under the influence of revolutionary "Third Wave" information technologies. Our population will become more mobile and diverse. Finally, longer life spans and improved health status will unleash a lifelong creative potential that was unimaginable up to now. At the same time, many hazards lie ahead. Large numbers of elders will have to depend on support from a younger generation, whose employment status is unsure. Debts, accumulated during the latter half of the 20th century, will have to be reckoned with, and even the promise of longevity is hollow if peoples' health status cannot keep pace while savings are eroded. It's a new world which also calls for new ideas, values, and attitudes.

Good Old Days?

History teaches that all great technological and economic transformations also unleash social and psychological turmoil as people struggle to adjust. Each setting has a specific set of values which makes good sense, even achieving the status of moral guidance. Think of the many children needed by an agricultural society plagued with high infant mortality rates. Fertility surely counted among the highest virtues then. A different set of values, headed by discipline in the work force, set the tone during the industrial era. Now, as we witness the dawn of the information age, the hallowed concept of "full employment" and the sacred forty-hour work week become relics of mid-20th century civilization. No wonder people are so confused.

If you've been following trends in the labor market, such as corporate downsizing and elimination of manufacturing sector jobs, you know how painful this can be to the individuals involved. It also explains the powerful appeal evoked by calls for a return to traditional values. According to opinion surveys, many people long for the past, even colonial days, thinking that our national greatness was built on lost virtues of piety, thrift, order, and self-reliance. Of all periods, the 1950s have the greatest nostalgic appeal: The world was still in order, families were happy, and everyone had a job with steadily-rising wages. More than a few national leaders hail the virtues of that era as the solution to problems of the future.

The truth, however, lies somewhere else. Historians, who have studied various epochs of our history, note that later generations build heroic myths about the past which tend to become enshrined as the "good old days," while conveniently forgetting the more unsavory aspects of that period. For example, the same folks who are appalled by the crime of "car-jacking" in suburban neighborhoods find sentimental pleasure in recalling stage coach robberies in the Old West. If you think about it, crime and violence are nothing new, but rather a central part of our historical tradition. Criminologists suggest that today's intense and sensational media coverage blows the issue out of proportion, creating an exaggerated sense of insecurity.

Now, cut to "family values." In her provocative recent book, *The Way We Never Were: American Families and the Nostalgia Trap*, family historian Stephanie Coontz reminds us that our ancestors had troubled families too. For instance, she explains that average colonial parents were harsh and remote to their children. Family support? The number of orphans and abandoned children tripled during the Civil War, crowding city streets with homeless youths. Other children were rented out as low-paid labor in sweatshops and mines as recently as a hundred years ago. During World War II, more than half of all teenagers dropped out of high school. Teen pregnancies proliferated in the nifty 50s; the response was "shot gun" weddings, often leading to divorce shortly thereafter.

Even the legendary prosperity of the 50s was a result of unique economic circumstances rather than the exemplary virtue of American people at the moment. Let's not forget that economic growth was mainly enjoyed by white—and blue-collar workers. In fact, Coontz notes that poverty rates at the time were quite high, and only post-Depression euphoria masked the genuine suffering of many deprived people.

Currently, it is fashionable to dote on the the hardships endured by our ancestors. At the same time, many believe that today's poor people are the victims of their own laziness and lack of initiative. Who would be willing to describe a Depression-era grandfather like that? Ultimately, it's foolish to say that the world would be better if people could only be more like their ancestors. Each period of history has its unique virtues and vices, neither of which can be resurrected. No, we simply can't turn back the clock.

Forecasting the 21st Century Life Cycle

From the standpoint of the individual, the life cycle phenomenon is quite instructive. Conventional wisdom teaches that normal people pass through various stages of life, usually classified as youth, adulthood, and old age. Defining and describing these stages or passages has been a major theme in the literature of psychology and sociology. In addition, a vast body of popular "self-help" literature is now available to assist us in mastering successive transitions. Unfortunately, most of it is limited to personal development and fails to address the dynamic, evolving world in which we live. That's where we need to look.

Experts in the field of human development are just starting to realize how much this century's unprecedented increase in longevity impacts the life cycle. While there is little or no change in childhood or youth, adulthood is now stretched far into the final period of old age, which itself lasts much longer. In essence, another third of a lifetime is being added to our existence. The issue, then, is one of redefining our values, lifestyles, and social institutions to accommodate this phenomenon. Gail Sheehy, who did much to raise popular awareness of the life cycle with her book *Passages* in 1976, highlighted life extension with the publication of *New Passages* in 1995. Sheehy noted that a forward shift of roughly ten years had occurred in peoples' lives between the years of 1950 and 1990. In other words, critical events such as marriage, child bearing, mid-life, and all subsequent developments are now possible ten years later than before. Others are already thinking in terms of a fifteen-year shift. The good news is that human potential is now vastly increased; the bad news is that many individuals feel out of sync, as the society around them continues to observe traditional, but outmoded, age distinctions.

Sheehy is not alone. Many other researchers come to the same conclusions. Lydia Bronte's recent book, *The Longevity Factor*, debunks the popular myth that people reach the pinnacle of achievement between the ages of 30 and 45. In fact, the truly productive period of life for many people in her study commenced at the age of 50. It no longer makes sense to compare ourselves to our parents or grandparents, since our potential for youth, vigor, and achievement extends far beyond their life experiences. Turn to Freda Rebelsky's book, *What Next?* A

Guide to Valued Aging and Other High Wire Adventures, if you want to learn about the many older individuals who defy the conventional wisdom of decline by launching themselves into new and exciting enterprises and activities. While not everyone has top flight capabilities, age should not bar human development. Finally, psychologist Dr. Ken Dychtwald offers a rousing salute to the human potential of a longer life span in his recent best seller, *Age Wave: The Challenges and Opportunities of an Aging America.*

All of this sounds great. So, what's the problem? In a nutshell, you could say that neither our values nor social and economic institutions have caught up with these evolving realities. Furthermore, the 21st century world of our forecast presents some daunting practical barriers, such as the impact of the information age on the labor market as well as careers and dwindling asset accumulation in the face of extended old age. Figure 1 illustrates that paradox: Even though life is being extended, men are leaving the work force at an earlier age. While the trend is not entirely voluntary, the consequences are disturbing for individuals and society alike. A few capable individuals will always transcend the limitations of their time; most of us, however, may end up saddled with a longer, but hardly more fulfilling, lifetime.

Surviving Information Age Overload and Uncluttering Life

If you're a connoisseur of classic cinema, you may recall Charlie Chaplin in *Modern Times*. More than half a century later, the images of a little man caught in the rapidly-spinning wheels of a mechanized, assembly-line society are still vivid. Well, the arrival of the information age is taking a similar toll on our lives. It appears that technological progress is happening faster and faster. Except for a few techno-nerds, most people are overwhelmed by the volume of information and communication coming their way. Business researchers have found that creative work in organizations declines as employees spend more of

Figure 1

Americans Age 65 and Older in the Civilian Labor Force by Gender, 1948-1994

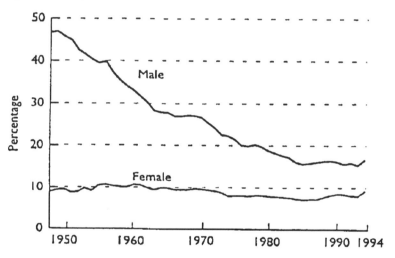

Source: U.S. Bureau of Labor Statistics. *Handbook on Labor Statistics*, Bulletin 2340 (Washington, DC: GPO, Aug. 1989), table 5; and *Employment and Earnings* vols. 37-41, table 3.

their time with various communication activities. We're drowning in data, because, while new technologies continue to proliferate, the old ones remain in place. In the past, I could have contacted you by letter and phone; nowadays, I can also reach you with a beeper, fax, e-mail, and who-knows-what next.

It is not only the volume, but also the instantaneous nature of the communication devices that can create anxiety. Remember too that these info-gadgets follow you home, where another battery of electronic entertainment and personal communication devices awaits you. If you're frazzled or consumed with the guilt of missing an e-mail from the boss, you're not alone. Psychologists are seeing more and more clients who are stressed out by overstimulation. In the long run, information technology developers of the 21st century will have to design equipment that is more "user friendly," which is to say that these high-powered electronic gadgets need to be tuned to our brains' processing and comprehension capacities. But what do you do until that happens? The experts advise people to seize control of the electronic world, rather than letting it control us. That means turning off the machines from time to time or claiming blocks of quiet time for "slow thinking" and reflection. Yoga, meditation, and exercise breaks are also recommended as stress therapy for the information age. Be creative. One busy account executive heads for the ladies room when things get too frantic. According to her, it's the one place where the phones don't ring, and you can gather your thoughts to resolve a problem in peace and quiet.

Information overload is a symptom of the growing complexity of life for many people. My eye doctor, a hard-charging, competent, and successful professional, is a good example. At my annual exam, we always compare notes on how life is treating us. For many years he proudly reported his growing stable of trophy possessions; even the sailboats got longer from year to year. Recently, however, the good doctor confessed his regret at once putting so much of life's energy into these material things.

They were a burden, and frankly, he was going to concentrate on more meaningful things like enjoying time with his wife and children.

According to the statistics, middle Americans are overloaded by consumer goods and creature comforts, yet see themselves struggling with maxed-out credit cards. While this sounds like nirvana for the retail business community, more and more people are seeking to simplify and unclutter their lives. Futurists have discovered an emerging culture of sophisticated rebels who are opting out of the compulsion to "own more stuff" and are concentrating on non-material values instead. It doesn't mean that they don't have or spend money. But instead of merchandise, these folks are choosing authentic, meaningful experiences, whether it be religious retreats, whale watching, or classical music performances. They are characterized by a high level of education, communal values, and a distrust of advertising. A good number of forecasters believe that mainstream culture in the 21st century, while technologically advancing, will feature a return to traditional human activities at the expense of virtual reality and other forms of perceptual manipulation.

Values and Attitudes for the 21st Century

Coming to terms with an unfamiliar and uncertain future is truly difficult. It takes genuine courage to discard outdated value concepts and move on to new ideas. That's not to say, of course, that the Ten Commandments and other historic moral precepts are no longer valid. Great traditions may be more valid than ever before and should be observed in the context of our evolving society. Rather, obsolete habits and customs will have to go. For instance, the concept of universal full-time employment currently measures the worth of an individual. Other criteria will have to be found to judge people in the robotic information age. Likewise, today's medical ethics seek to prolong human life at all costs; if left unchallenged, evolving technology could well turn our health care facilities into storage areas for comatose centenarians.

Creating appropriate values for the 21st century is a task for both individuals and society. Let us begin with the personal perspective. It starts with your appreciation and understanding of the future world, as described in various chapters of this book. Then consider some personal objectives which make sense. Next, use forecasting techniques, like those described in Chapter 1, to project some realistic and likely scenarios. If the prospects are less than encouraging, it's high time to reconsider. One approach is to re-examine your personal values; can they be maintained and validated in the next century? For example, most folks still operate on the principle of a "linear" life, where events follow a clearly defined, chronological path. Deviance constitutes failure. We now know that the future holds less regimented, cyclic life patterns where personal and professional lives progress according to a less orderly but still logical rhythm. Once you accept this, the final step is to prepare by investing in your future. We know that this includes such components as continued learning, being your own doctor, building adequate financial resources, and other tools of mastery discussed in previous chapters.

America's Future: Community or Free-For-All?

Future values for society are more difficult to determine. For one thing, American democracy seeks to accommodate a vast range of different ideas about the proper relation of people to society. Much of our greatness is based on the idea that different individuals and groups should be allowed to determine their own destinies. On the other hand, we are ambivalent about our sense of community. Do we share common bonds of mutual obligation, requiring that prosperous elements of society share their bounty with those in need? Obviously, there's a broad spectrum of sentiment on that issue. According to opinion polls, trend setting Baby Boomers have developed a strong sense of individualism and personal freedom. It's a jungle out there, and you must be strong to survive. Or think of it in terms of "looking out for number one." While such values supported the upward mobility of successful individuals, America's evolving economic and social environment seems to call for greater commitment to community needs. Why?

Mainstream economists are concerned that, as our economy continues its transition from manufacturing to information and services, the number of "good" jobs will continue to decline and create economic hardships for millions of Americans. It's easy to get confused about these trends. On the one hand, there'll always be a shortage of technical experts who command high pay. Meanwhile, government statistics also show that real wages for the majority of working people have been falling since the mid-70s. As this wage-earning middle class gets thinned out, people will cluster more and more on the extremes of the income distribution scale. While jobs are still plentiful in the service sector, a closer look will show that the prevailing wages are scarcely sufficient for a decent standard of living or raising a family. Social problems are sure to follow.

"Fend for Yourself!" may have worked on the frontier, but it makes no sense in a crowded, urban, industrial society. Popular solutions such as giving the poor and unemployed a swift kick in the pants, or presenting each with a lap top computer, fail to recognize the basic truth that traditional employment will continue to decline. We're not talking about "Mc Jobs," but about full-time positions which offer hospitalization, retirement plans, and other benefits. How can we expect women to participate in the work force without providing adequate and reasonably-priced child care? If the social and economic rules of the machine age no longer apply, we must come up with some very creative solutions to occupy people's time, while offering them a decent standard of living. As things stand, the technological revolution becomes a double-edged sword; it reduces the need for human labor, which, in turn, creates the potential for a very narrow and elitist society.

Unless the bountiful fruits of the information society are

shared, non-participants will need to rely on their own devices, namely crime and other forms of anti-social behavior. Modern Brazil, where huge masses of desperately poor people menace a tiny elite, is one scenario. Wealthy people surround themselves with armed guards and live in barbed-wire enclaves. Is America headed in the same direction? A number of influential futurists point toward renewed segregation along socioeconomic lines in the next century. They suggest that upwardly mobile people are increasingly abandoning public facilities in favor of private enclaves for themselves and their offspring. Consider what is happening in American education. The noticeable growth of private schools probably has more to do with social exclusivity than academic standards. For many years, public schools served the useful purpose of allowing people from different racial and social backgrounds to mingle and develop tolerances for their respective differences. In the future, our local schools may well become the dumping grounds for those who get "selected out" or are unable to come up with private school fees. Why should upper income tax payers want to support such institutions?

Similar trends are evident in residential patterns. More and more "gated communities" with protective walls and security systems have started to make their appearance in America's once open and inviting suburbs. Security experts suggest that high walls don't always provide the desired security. In the long run, these symbols of wealth and privilege are more likely to generate envy and resentment among the have-nots; criminal elements will regard them as magnets for exploitation. As the divisions between rich and poor segments of society grow, our nation's sense of community and civility will disappear, giving way to a dark world of strife and disorder. Is this the wave of the future? Think about it.

Your Legacy: The Ultimate Future Investment

The concept of legacy normally refers to what we inherit from our ancestors. Family histories bear witness to the hard work and sacrifice of earlier generations. In a larger sense, our prosperous society owes much to previous generations who built the foundation. In the case of America, the nation's ultimate stature owes much to the hardships and tribulations endured by the early settlers. We can be justly proud of this heritage.

Let's not forget, however, that we, too, are building a heritage for future generations. History is not about to end, and our generation will be remembered for whatever grief or benefit gets passed on to those who succeed us. Earlier chapters of this book stressed how individuals needed to invest in themselves to master the future. In the long run, we must also consider the needs of future generations. It's only fair to those who preceded us.

How, then, do we invest in the future? The basic concept, you will remember, involves saving, or delaying present expenditures to serve some greater future good. Think of the man who plants a hardwood sapling, knowing that he will never enjoy the shade of the mature tree. At the individual level, it means caring for one's children and family members, seeing that they receive adequate health care, education, and other preparation for life. On the larger scale, we also bear a responsibility for the future welfare of the society at large. Investments here might include contributions to the preservation of the environment, culture, education, and the many other things which shape a better future world. Think of creating enduring value, and your heritage will be a worthy one.

TO LEARN MORE

Chapter 1

Edward Cornish, ed. Exploring Your Future: Living, Learning and Working in the life style, World Future Society, 1996

Marvin Cetron & Owen Davies, *Probable Tomorrows: How Science and Technology will Transform our Lives in the Next Twenty Years* , St. Martin's Press, 1997

Paul C. Light, *Baby Boomers,* Norton, 1988

Charles F. Longino, Jr. "Myths of an Aging America," *American Demographics*, August, 1994

Oliver W. Markley and Walter R. McCuan, eds., *America beyond 2001: Opposing Viewpoints,* Greenhaven Press, 1996

John Naisbitt, *Megatrends 2000* , Morrow, 1990

Cheryl Russell, *100 Predictions for the Baby Boomers*, Plenum Press, 1987

Alvin & Heidi Toffler, *Creating a New Civilization: The Politics of the Third Wave,*
Turner Publishing, 1994

Chapter 2

Stanley Aronowitz and William DiFazio, *The Jobless Future: Sci-Tech and the Dogma of Work,* University of Minnesota Press, 1994

Robert Barner, *Lifeboat Strategies: How to Keep Your Career Above Water During Tough Times—Or Any Time*, AMACOM, 1994

William Bridges, *Job Shift: How to Prosper in a Workplace without Jobs,* Addison Wesley, 1994

Joseph Coates, et. al. *Future Work: Seven Critical Forces Reshaping Work and the Work Force in North America,* Jossey-Bass, 1990

Edward Cornish, ed. *Careers Tomorrow: The Outlook for Work in a Changing World,* World Future Society, 1988

Harry S. Dent, Jr., *Job Shock: Four New Principles Transforming our Work and Business*, St. Martins Press, 1995

Kenneth C. Gray and Edwin L. Herr, *Other Ways to Win: Creating Alternatives for High School Graduates*, Corwin Press (Sage), 1995

Helen Harkness, *The Career Chase: Taking Creative Control in a Chaotic Age,* Davies-Black, 1997.

Andy Hines, "Jobs and Infotech: Work in the Information Society," *The Futurist,* January/February, 1994

Ronald L. and Caryl Rae Krannich, *The Best Jobs for the 1990s and into the 21st Century,* Impact Publications, 1995

Thomas S. Moore, *The Disposable Workforce*, Aldine de Gruyter, 1996

Jeremy Rifkin, ***The End of Work***, Tarcher/Putnam, 1995

Chapter 3

American Association of Retired People, *Think of Your Future: Retirement Planning Workbook,* 1988 and later editions

Karen Ferguson and Kate Blackwell, *The Pension Book*, Arcade, 1995

Peter E. Gaudio and Virginia Nicols, *Your Retirement Benefits*, Wiley, 1992

Craig S. Karple, *The Retirement Myth*, Harper-Collins, 1995

Daniel Kehrer, *12 Steps to a Worry-Free Retirement*, Kiplinger Books, 1995

Eric R. Kingson & James H. Schultz, eds., *Social Security in the 21st Century*, Oxford University Press, 1996

Robert K. Otterbourg, *Retire and Thrive*, Kiplinger Books, 1995

James Schulz, *The Economics of Aging*, Auburn House, 1992

Eric Schurenberg, *401k: Take Charge of Your Future*, Warner, 1996

Chapter 4

Robert B. Coplan, et.al., *Ernst & Young's Total Financial Planner*, Wiley, 1997

Frank Feather, *The Future Consumer*, Warwick, 1994

David & Tom Gardner, *The Motley Fool Investment Guide*, Simon & Schuster, 1996

Gregory Georgiou, *Investing in the Technologies of Tomorrow: Discovering the Super Companies of the 21st Century*, Probus, 1994

Carole Gould, *New York Times Guide to Mutual Funds,* Times Books, 1992

Andrew Leckey, *Investing for the 21st Century*, World Future Society, 1995 (also found in July/August 1995 issue of *The Futurist*

Marshall Loeb, *Marshall Loeb's Lifetime Financial Strategies*, 1996

John Naisbitt, *Megatrends Asia*, Simon & Schuster, 1996

Lester Thurow, T*he Future of Capitalism: How Today's Economic Forces Shape Tomorrow's Economic World,* Morrow, 1996

Don Tapscott, *The Digital Economy: Promise and Peril in the Age of Networked Intelligence* McGraw-Hill, 1996

Chapter 5

Henry J. Aaron, *Serious and Unstable Condition: Financing America's Health Care*, Institution, 1991

Clement Bezold and Erica Mayer, eds. *Future Care; Responding to the Demand for Change,* Faulkner & Gray, 1996

D. Callahan, *Setting Limits: Medical Goals in an Aging Society*, Simon & Schuster, 1995

Marilyn Moon, *Medicare Now and in the Future*, Urban Institute, 1996

Kant Patel and Mark E. Rushefsky, *Health Care Politics and Policy in America*, M.E. Sharpe, 1995

Alice M. Rivlin and Joshua Wiener, *Caring for Disabled Elderly: Who Will Pay?* Brookings Institution, 1988

Les Seplaki, *Cost and Competition in American Medicine*, University Press of America, 1995

U.S. Congressional Research Service, *Medical Source Book: Background Data and Analysis,* U.S. Government Printing Office, 1993

Health Care in America: Opposing Viewpoints, Greenhaven Press, 1994

Chapter 6

American Heart Association & American Cancer Association, *Living Well, Staying Well*, Times Books, 1996

Anthology, *Health and Fitness: Opposing Viewpoints,* Greenhaven Press, 1996

Jean Barilla, ed., *The Nutrition Superbook: Vol. 1 The Antioxidants*, Keats Publishing, 1995

Harvey and Marilyn Diamond, *Fit for Life I & II*, Warner Books, 1987

P. Ebersole and P. Hess, *Toward Healthy Aging,* Mosby, 1990

Editors of Consumer Reports, *The New Medicine Show: Consumer Union's New Practical Guide to Everyday Health Poblems and Health .Poducts,* Consumer Union, 1989

Leonard Hayflick, *How and Why We Age,* Ballantine, 1996

Sherwin B. Nuland, *How We Die*, Vintage, 1993

Chapter 7

Editors of Kiplinger Publications, *Buying and Selling a Home*, Kiplinger Books, 1993

Alice and Fred Lee, *The 50 Best Retirement Communities in America*, St. Martin's 1994

Charles Longino, *Retirement Migration in America*, Vacation Publications, 1995

David Savageau, *Retirement Places Rated*, Prentice Hall, 1990

William Seavy, *Moving to a Small Town*, Dearborn Financial Publishing, 1996

Conclusion

Lydia Bronte, *The Longevity Factor,* Harper-Collins, *1993*

Stephanie Coontz, T*he Way We Never Were: American Families and the Nostalgia Trap*, Basic Books, 1992

Ken Dychtwald, Age Wave: *The Challenges and Opportunities of an Aging America,* Tarcher, 1989

Gail Sheehy, *New Passages: Mapping Your Life Across Time*, Ballantine Books, 1995